MEN OF MAGNA CARTA: Right, Might and Depravity

BY

DANIEL FORBES

Published 2015

ISBN 978-0-692-41288-6

Daniel Forbes
208 Cedar St
Sanford, MI 48657

mistrhistre@yahoo.com

© Copyright: No portion of this work may be reproduced for any reason or for any purpose except small portions as part of a literary review without expressed permission of the author and publisher, Daniel Forbes, or his assigns.

Acknowledgements

My mother, Joan R. Forbes McWatters, encouraged my interest in history. What a gift! At Wauseon High School, Jane Reed started me on the road of writing. My thanks! Various history professors at Central Michigan University guided me in doing serious research as I earned my Master's degree. Invaluable! The ladies at the reference desk at the Grace A. Dow Memorial Library found books for me from across the nation--even one from a far away Oregon monastery. Wow! My friend, Shirley Marsteller, edited my work from retirement in Florida. (Sorry for my persistent errors!) My artistic friends Lisa Grove (cover art) and Marilyn Garrison (portraits) gave me gifts from their talents. I value these. The people who invented and made available "spell check"--without that...Oh my! And most of all, to my wonderful, beautiful, patient, encouraging wife, Cheryl, I owe everything. Thank You!

TABLE OF CONTENTS

WHAT SAY THE REEDS AT RUNNYMEDE?

CHAPTER		PAGE
1	MAGNA WHAT?	12
2	CORONATION CHARTER	18
3	STEPHEN LANGTON	31
4	THUNDERING TONGUE	43
5	...AND A SCHOLAR	57
6	KING JOHN AND ELEANOR	62
7	GREATEST KNIGHT	76
8	KING JOHN REIGNS	88
9	RUNNYMEDE CONFRONTATION	100
10	AFTER RUNNYMEDE	108
11	POSTSCRIPT	116
APPENDIX		119

1100 TEXT CORONATION CHARTER	119
1215 TEXT MAGNA CARTA	122
1217 TEXT MAGNA CARTA	136
1217 FOREST CHARTER	146
BIBLIOGRAPHY	153

WHAT SAY THE REEDS AT RUNNYMEDE?

Rudyard Kipling (1865-1936)

At Runnymede, at Runnymede,
What say the reeds at Runnymede?
The lissom reeds that give and take,
That bend so far, but never break,
They keep the sleepy Thames awake
With tales of John at Runnymede.

At Runnymede, at Runnymede,
Oh, hear the reeds at Runnymede:
'You musn't sell, delay, deny,
A freeman's right or liberty.
It wakes the stubborn Englishry,
We saw 'em roused at Runnymede!

When through our ranks the Barons came,
With little thought of praise or blame,
But resolute to play the game,
They lumbered up to Runnymede;
And there they launched in solid line
The first attack on Right Divine,
The curt uncompromising "Sign!"
They settled John at Runnymede.

At Runnymede, at Runnymede,
Your rights were won at Runnymede!
No freeman shall be fined or bound,
Or dispossessed of freehold ground,
Except by lawful judgment found

And passed upon him by his peers.
Forget not, after all these years,
The Charter signed at Runnymede.'

And still when mob or Monarch lays
Too rude a hand on English ways,
The whisper wakes, the shudder plays,
Across the reeds at Runnymede.
And Thames, that knows the moods of kings,
And crowds and priests and suchlike things,
Rolls deep and dreadful as he brings
Their warning down from Runnymede!

Chapter 1

MAGNA WHAT?

For most Americans the Magna Carta is a term for something or other they think they learned about in high school. They may know that it is a document having something to do with government. Most see little connection between their daily lives and some document written in Latin eight hundred years ago. This is the story of the men who wrote the Magna Carta and shepherded it through to acceptance and importance.

So why are they important, why is the document important?

The world of 1215 was different than our world today when it comes to technology, social structures, communication and many other things. However, there is one thing that really has not changed through history.

Human nature is the same now as it was hundreds, even thousands of years ago. People are selfish, mean and hungry for power. If a person has the opportunity to grab power, to increase that power, to use that power for selfish enjoyment, they will do exactly that--unless there is something to inhibit or control them. We see that today in the stories of government or business or international or local neighborhoods, when a person or group takes the opportunities they have to lord over others. They may use military force, or legal maneuvers, or personal threats to get their way. On the other hand, the victims of this power grab tend to resist.

Sometimes they resist in order to compete with the aggressor to take his place, and sometimes they resist because they believe there are injustices that need to be made right. History is filled with stories of these kinds of situations. Occasionally, somebody creates or recreates a way to stem the tide of evil in society so that there is another barrier for potential lords to overcome. Sometimes these impediments last a very long time, and we enjoy the protection thus created. The Magna Carta is one such impediment to restrict evil in society. Stephen Langton and William Marshal were the men who put it into position. Every day we are protected by the provisions of the Magna Carta.

    Americans live under "the Supreme Law of the Land" known as the United States Constitution. Our constitution is a document born out of circumstances and previous events of history. The events of the early 13th century that created the Magna Carta are part of that story, so now we expect that the laws we follow and the rights we enjoy are written down. When one of us purchases something at a store, buys a car, or a house, we have certain assurances supported by law. We have Constitutional protection concerning our property rights. If a local street gang would steal our purchase, that is illegal, and we can expect that the police will try to recover our property and return it to us. If some level of the government tried to take our house away from us for whatever reason, they are prohibited--except by "due process of law". This idea of protecting property rights from being taken without "due process" is an inheritance we received from the Magna Carta. In 1215 the particulars of how the government took people's possessions was different than today, but the basic principle is the same. If we should decide to stand up for our rights, we would consult the laws written down about our situation. Magna Carta was an early example of how the King of England was restricted by laws written down. We take these things for granted--and it is a huge blessing that we can do so. It seems like every generation must, however, reassert their roadblocks and barriers against those who would take the property and freedoms away from them. We must restrict the power which the power hungry wish to gain to themselves.

There are other rights we inherit from the Magna Carta. Our First Amendment to the Constitution guarantees freedom of religion. The Magna Carta more than once stated that the Church would be free from government interference. The exact meaning of the Constitution and the "Great Charter" (the translated meaning of "Magna Carta") are different, for the historical conditions in 1215 and over 550 years later in America were not the same. Yet the principle remains that it is wrong for the government and religion to be inappropriately entangled and these documents address that.

The Charter put limitations on what the King of England was allowed to do. The trend in European countries was for the Kings to get increasingly more powerful--except in England where the kings were more and more restricted. The Magna Carta put a group of twenty-five barons over the decisions of the King and created yet another body of noblemen to enforce the resulting decisions. This was the start of the Parliamentary system of government in England. While the U.S. does not have a Parliament it does have an elected body of officials to oversee the actions of the President as Parliament checks the power of the King.

This Great Council was to restrict the taxing power of the King, according to the Charter, in a way similar to the U.S. House of Representatives having the only authority to initiate tax laws under the Constitution. It would be difficult to weigh the importance of this shift in the "power of the purse" from being held by the king to being held by the Council. This trend would grow after the Magna Carta, but it began with this Charter.

In England the people had long had the right to have a trial before their property, liberty or life could be taken. They had enjoyed this right thanks to the years of Roman rule, but the Romans left Britain in 410, and over the years, this right had been eroded. Magna Carta put it back in the forefront, written down for all to see. The Constitution likewise makes our "due process' rights known in Article 3, section 2.

We take our standard weights and measures for granted. A pound is a certain unchanging weight and a gallon is a gallon. The Great Charter sets down this principle that is such a great encouragement of trade and healthy business interactions. Article 1, section 8 of the Constitution does the same. Both documents give the power to coin money to the government.

Clause 20 of the Magna Carta addresses the issue of fines for breaking the law. It says essentially that the fine or penalty should fit the crime and that a person should not be penalized so heavily that he would be deprived of the ability to make a living. Also on the topic of crimes, both the Constitution and the Charter say that no person shall be put on trial for a crime unless there is credible evidence, credible witnesses. Credibility is emphasized as the barons had experienced situations where people were put on trial for offenses that had no fair evidence to support the charge. Some writers would have us believe that the Magna Carta did not apply to the general citizens of England, but this is wrong. Yes, some of the provisions of the Charter applied to the nobles, but many also applied to "my whole kingdom" and to "everyone".

We have seen that many of the rights we enjoy have a root in the 800 year old document known as the

Magna Carta, or Great Charter. It is extremely important for us to know these historical connections, because history gives us appreciation and perspective on our lives today. We would be open to abuse more quickly if we were not aware of where our rights came from and the circumstances under which we got those rights. No one person is capable of creating such a document as Magna Carta or the Constitution. The political environment had to be right, but there did need to be at least one leader who saw the vision for what could be, and who had an idea how to reach that vision. That extraordinary person in the early 13th Century was Stephen Langton. He was assisted in this work by the warrior William Marshal. Their foil was the hated monarch, King John. This book is about these three men and those who influenced them, as well as a recounting of how the Magna Carta came to be written.

Chapter 2

THE CORONATION CHARTER

The story of the Magna Carta began about one hundred fifty years before it was written. In 1066 Edward the Confessor king of England died without children, and William, Duke of Normandy, believed he had a right to the English throne. There were other claimants, so he had to conquer England to make his claim good. When William the Conqueror died, he left Normandy to his eldest son, Robert Curthose. "Curthose" indicates that he was a short man. His second son, William II (called William Rufus--"Rufus" because his hair was red), inherited England. The Conqueror's third son, Henry received no land, but did receive a large sum of money.

William Rufus was not a popular king in England. Like his father, he ruled with energy and a very heavy hand. His favorites received lands and castles while those not favored were deprived of their lands. Taxes were heavy and many. Additionally, Rufus was known as "a mocker and a blasphemer...one who took a strange pleasure in dealing with his maker as a personal enemy." While this alone would not have made William unique in European history it was unusual in England especially so soon after the reign of Edward the Confessor who was known for his humility and piety. William Rufus offended the noblemen of England who were spiritually minded. However, there were many clergy--especially at the higher levels of Church leadership--who were more interested in gaining political favors from the king and would overlook his lack of piety.

The Catholic Church of the middle ages had become quite wealthy. Knights and noblemen nearing the end of their lives, wished to reconcile themselves to God before they died, and they tended to give gifts to the Church. Gifts of money and land were turned over to monasteries and local churches in hopes that the monks and priests there would pray for the soul of the one giving the gifts. Over time large portions of the country were owned by the Church, so the Bishops and Abbots became the holders of significant wealth. If the King should require men to fight a war, he would need the backing of these same Bishops in order to be successful, as each holding of land needed to supply a certain number of foot soldiers and knights. They would also be expected to contribute significant financial aid as well. What this all meant was that the individual who was named to be Bishop was politically powerful and important to the King, as well as to the Pope.

The Pope at that time was under the control of a faction led by Hildebrand who was part of the Cluny Reform which began in 910. The Cluny reform had spread to thousands of monasteries and influenced the thinking of a large number of clergy in Europe. The reformers stressed piety of life, celibacy (refusal to marry), education for clergy and the supremacy of the Pope over not only the Church but over laymen such as kings. The Cluny reformers were very strongly against "lay investiture" or the practice of kings "investing" (appointing) Bishops. The reformers wanted the Pope to make these appointments to ensure that their spiritual qualifications would lift the general spirituality of the church toward godliness. Kings, on the other hand, wanted Bishops who were personally loyal to them, and who had military and administrative skills to further the political agenda of the king. Bishops had been appointed by kings for hundreds of years, and they would not easily surrender this power. The "lay investiture" controversy was the dominant political issue in Europe during the Middle Ages. Wealth and power were the prizes for the side that won this battle.

King William Rufus was not on the side of the Cluny reform, and seemed to enjoy conflict with the Church. Rufus took his opposition to the Church to an even greater extreme than demanding the right of investiture. He was a blasphemer. He was homosexual. Even nobles who were not particularly religious found Rufus to be abhorrent. Rebellion against such a man had a high likelihood of being approved, or at least ignored, by the Pope.

Another Church reform movement in Europe was less formal than the Cluny reform, but regarding Normandy and England perhaps even stronger. The monastery at Bec, in Normandy, created a fellowship of church leaders that influenced churches in both regions. The Bec ideology stressed scripture, logical arguments and charity. It was a fraternity of personal friendships rather than a formal order or rule. Key early supporters of the Bec monastery were members of the Clare family, Richard Fitzgilbert and Walter Gifford. The Clare family remained involved in the Bec movement for several generations.

The Clares also had been close advisors to William Conqueror. But when William Rufus came to the throne, they were not treated as well as they were accustomed. On one occasion Gilbert and Roger Clare had warned Rufus about a plan to ambush him. The guilty plotters had been caught and killed, but the Clares had not been rewarded. On another occasion a different plot was exposed by the Clares, but on that occasion the Clares were suspected of being a party to the plot, and though forgiven by Rufus a barrier was elected between the men. One of the rebellions was led by Robert of Meulan who also served as a close advisor to the King's brother Henry.

A key leader of the Bec reform was Anselm. In 1093 William Rufus allowed the abbots of Canterbury to select Anselm as Archbishop of Canterbury--however this was four years after the previous Archbishop had died. In the interval the King has taken the income from Canterbury for himself and of course profited handsomely from that. Anselm, a premier eleventh century theologian, supported both the Bec and Cluny reform movements, and that led to conflict with William Rufus. By 1097 Rufus forced Anselm's exile from England. Rufus probably knew but did not care that he was creating a growing list of enemies. These enemies eventually acted against him.

The youngest of William Conqueror's sons, Henry, was born in England, where he spent most of his childhood. He probably received his education there as well, possibly from Gundulf, Bishop of Rochester, a Bec monk and friend of Anselm. In 1088 Henry purchased about a third of Normandy from his eldest brother, Robert Curthose, who was raising money to attack William Rufus in the hope he could gain the crown in England, given William's unpopularity. Rufus put down the rebellion as he was a highly competent general, and when Rufus invaded Normandy in 1091, Henry lost his Norman holding, and was exiled from both Normandy and England for a time. It is possible that while traveling Henry visited Scotland and met his future wife Edith.

Edith was daughter of King Malcolm of Scotland and Margaret niece of Edward Confessor who had ruled

England before the Conqueror. Margaret was a devout Christian who was later sainted. Margaret was an active model to her children, taking a significant role in their upbringing and early education. Later Edith was sent to a convent for an education--first at Romsey then at Wilton. Both places were known for the excellence of education offered to girls, and Margaret's sister was Prioress at Romsey. There is a story told about Edith bathing and kissing the feet of lepers when her brother David discovered her. He reprimanded Edith, but she rebuked him for it. David wrote that "I had not yet come to know the Lord, nor had His spirit been revealed to me..."--suggesting that he admitted he was wrong to reprimand his sister, and that Edith did have a relationship with the Lord which David would later acquire.

In 1093, King Malcolm and his eldest son David raided into northern England where both were killed. Three days later an already ill Margaret also died. Edgar Atheling Margaret's brother went from England, where he was under the protection and authority of William Rufus to Scotland, to take Edith and her sister to safety until the successor for King of Scotland was decided. It is unknown where Edith was between 1093 and 1100, but she may have spent time in Rufus's court and at Wilton. Kings tended to "decorate" their court with beautiful young women of the noble class. Henry was also occasionally at Rufus's court, and the two may well have become acquainted. One contemporary said Edith was the woman "to whom he (Henry) had long been attracted", and another calls her "the maiden whose perfection of character he had long adored". Henry may have experienced a spiritual change as one writer said that, "his spirituality was marked by a strong, almost morbid awareness of sin and the need for repentance".

Henry and Edith may have found common ground for political, spiritual as well as romantic reasons. It was perhaps during this interval that Edith's name was changed to Matilda, a name sounding more French, the language of the Norman kings.

    William Rufus was at the height of his power. Robert Curthose had gone on the First Crusade where he had experienced success, and Rufus could hope that he would not return. Rufus was forty years old and in excellent health. He was going hunting, one of his favorite pastimes. Hunts usually began in the morning, but this day the hunt began after noon--possibly because of too much drinking the night before. The hunting party, invited to the hunt by the King, broke up into pairs and set out for the wood to await the game that would be driven toward the hunters by others. Walter Tirel, a cousin of the Clare brothers and excellent marksman, was with the King. "Someone" shot a single arrow that entered the chest of William Rufus, and he fell from his horse driving the arrow deeper. He was dead, "accidentally killed" while hunting.

    Immediately events went into motion. Walter Tirel fled to the coast of England where he was fortunate enough to find a ship. He did not stop until he was securely in France. The Clare brothers were on the hunt as were various Clare relatives, but they did not raise a general alarm until morning. Prince Henry was not with the hunters, though he was in England. When he heard of the death of his brother, he went directly to Winchester to secure the treasury for himself. Late the next day William Rufus was buried at Winchester. Few mourned. He had died "without repentance...no bell tolled, no prayer said, no alms given for the soul...whose damnation was taken for granted by all men." Henry was present at the burial. Immediately the barons met to acclaim Henry as King. There were dissenters who favored Robert Curthose the older brother and who was rumored to be returned from the crusade but he would not return to Normandy for another month. Others argued that the peace of England could not afford to wait and besides that, Curthose was a foreigner. This faction won out. Henry headed to Westminster where Thomas, Archbishop of York crowned him. The new king, Henry I accepted loyalty oaths from his barons, issued a meaningless general coronation charter promising to enforce good laws and abolish bad ones.

He ordered the arrest of Rufus' notorious advisor Ranulf Flambard, but not the arrest of Walter Tirel the probable assassin of William Rufus. Henry issued an invitation for Anselm to return to Canterbury from exile.

He also dealt with several charters and appointments relating to churches across the country that Rufus had ignored so that he could financially benefit from their wealth. One of the main supporters of Curthose for King was appointed Bishop of Winchester, and one of the Clare brothers was appointed Abbot of Ely. It is possible that Henry began the process of arranging his marriage to Matilda (Edith) at this time (August 1100).

With rumors circulating about the untimely death of Rufus and the hint that he had been assassinated not shot accidentally, Henry desperately needed the full support of the nobility and the people of England. His reputation as being overly sexually active was not a help either--at that point he had fathered about twenty illegitimate children whom he acknowledged. He needed a good marriage--a marriage to a Saxon princess would be a huge political advantage. Edith/Matilda was then at the convent in Wilton.

Archbishop Anselm summoned her to discuss the proposed marriage.

Was she a nun? If so, of course no marriage could occur. She told the story of her intended marriage to Alan of Scotland, and the death of her father and brother at the hands of the Normans, and the disruption of her life at that time. She told about her residencies in convents as a way to avoid the unwanted advances of various Norman barons--that she wore the habit of a nun only to thwart these advances. Would she marry the Norman Henry? Their ages were very close to one another, a rare occurrence for royal marriages, and they probably knew each other already. Matilda's future was uncertain, and this proposal was the best she could hope for, and she agreed--but she attached a string. As a grandniece of the revered King Edward the Confessor, and daughter of the soon to be sainted Margaret of Scotland, Matilda possessed the moral and circumstantial clout to require a powerful concession from Henry--the document known as the Coronation Charter of Henry I (1100), the basis of the Magna Carta. This charter restricted many significant powers of the King (you may choose to read it in the appendix of this book). He would have little reason to voluntarily agree to these restrictions on his own. Henry had been taught to use "soft affectionate words, delay and subtle maneuvers behind the scene" to avoid unpleasant commitments, so it is most likely that he was forced to sign this second charter of his coronation with no intention to follow it, though he may have had a say in writing it.

The Charter is written as fourteen paragraphs called chapters some of which are single sentences. In print the whole document including witnesses, takes only two pages. However the content and wording display evidence of careful thought. Chapter one announced that Henry had been crowned King of England "by the mercy of God (and by) the common counsel of the barons of the whole of England". In fact, there were few barons present when he was chosen, but the appeal to God and the barons shows that he is not King by conquest or self-appointment. His charter next indicates that the King was going to correct the wrong done to the kingdom through oppressive taxes, and that the Church would be free. Henry promised that he would not steal from the church as William Rufus notoriously had. The chapter also gave hope that there would be further reforms like the ones Henry had already implemented.

Under Rufus, heirs could receive the lands of their fathers only by paying what amounted to a bribe to the king. Chapter two promised this would no longer be the practice, but payments would be under the principle of justice and legitimacy. This protection was made applicable to sub-vassals also.

Chapters three and four were each nearly as long as the first chapter and both apply to rights of women. These chapters seem to show that Matilda had a hand in writing the charter. The fact that Magna Carta repeats these rights demonstrates that over one hundred years of practice separating the two charters did not end the problems addressed. The third chapter promised that fathers could arrange the marriage of their daughters to whom they wished, along with land as dowry, as long as they discussed the situation with the king and the arrangement was not with an enemy of the king. This chapter also stated that a widow without children could refuse a marriage arranged by the king in consultation with his barons, and she could keep her dowry. The fourth chapter pledged that a widow who survived her children would not be forced into a marriage, and that the widow could be guardian of her children if they still lived. The barons were also under the same restrictions. These chapters gave women a glimmer of legal rights in an environment where women had very few rights.

Chapter five deals with currency. Henry eliminated a tax "which did not exist in the time of King Edward." The tax was on the currency itself, but the Charter promises justice if anyone including makers of money, were guilty of money tampering. These people were called "moneyers". The making of currency was not yet the function of government, but an individual could purchase a punch die to punch out coins from a sheet of silver and actually create money as a business. The coins were required to weigh a standard amount and bear the images the king required, and the moneyer could have a hand cut off if he cheated. Since the value of the silver was less than the face value of the coins as all money is, there was profit to be made as a moneyer. However a tax on the number of coins made, squeezed that profit to nearly nothing at all especially when the price of silver rose.

Chapters six through eight dealt with debts owed for inheritances and bribes paid to Rufus. All these were pardoned though rents and payments for the sake of others were still in effect. The barons received the right to make a will, but if there were no will, his widow children and liegemen (lesser nobles under his authority) would have a say. Chapter nine eliminated a fine that made a difference between Normans and Englishmen in the case of murder so that national distinction became less important.

Chapter ten unlike all the others proclaims that there would be no change from Norman practice. The Forest laws implemented since the Conquest would remain.
These laws were very much hated by the English, but the hunt was so important to Normans that no changes

would be made. Before the Norman Conquest there were no designated "forests", but after the conquest, forests were created as the private hunting preserves of the king. Normal people were not allowed to enter the forest to hunt, gather wood for their fires, or any other reason. Occasionally entire villages were ordered to be abandoned because it was in a "forest". Some forests were actually grass lands. Henry is known to have imported exotic animals, and he kept them in a forest at Woodstock, creating what amounted to a zoo/private game preserve.

Chapter eleven eliminated taxes on lands held by knights who were in the military service of the king. This made it easier for knights to provide themselves with horses and arms and thus be more effective in the defense of the kingdom.

Chapter twelve says, "I establish my firm peace throughout the whole kingdom and command that it be henceforth maintained." Henry excelled at keeping the peace. The contrast between his benevolent and wise administration and the administrations of both of his brothers is striking.

Chapter thirteen defined what the king meant by "peace". He promised to restore the laws of Edward as amended by William Conqueror. There were certain properties that had been taken from the Crown upon the death of Rufus. Chapter fourteen promises amnesty to all who returned that property, and for those who did not should return the property, but stiff fines were promised.

The Coronation Charter of Henry I is a marvel of insight, foresight and wisdom. It has been observed that Magna Carta is simply an updating and repeat of this Coronation Charter. Nothing new was added in principle in the Magna Carta. The reign of Henry I was marked by wisdom, and the creation of an improved more accessible legal system. Matilda ruled England for her husband when he was away in Normandy-- a frequent occurrence. She is one of very few women who ruled a nation as agent of her husband while he lived. Normally a highly trusted baron would take that function. It is a testament to the trust Henry had in his wife, and to the intelligence and wisdom she possessed. The leading reform institutions of Cluny and Bec monasteries knew Henry and Matilda for their bountiful gifts; however these reforms did not fully accomplish their intended goals although they maintained a certain ideal of righteous living for Church leaders.

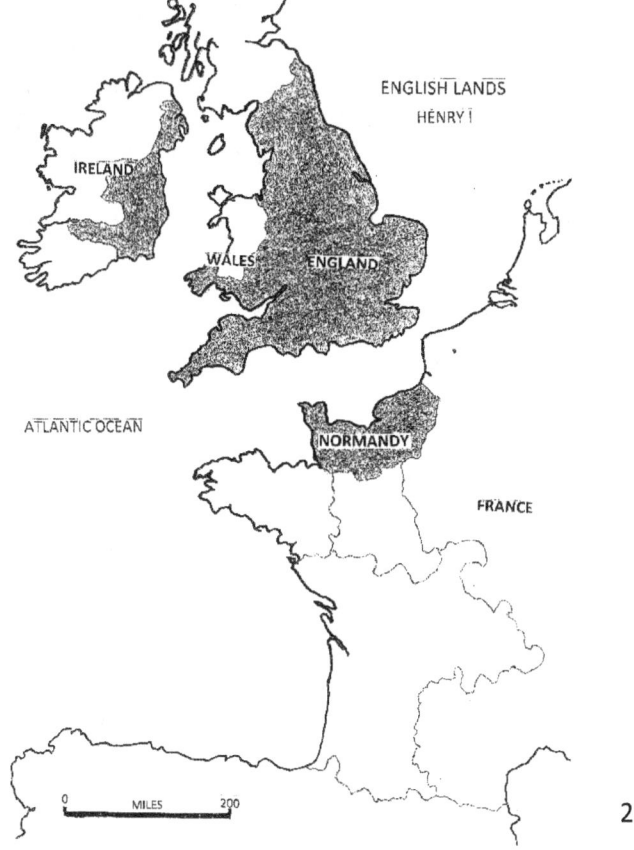

Chapter 3

STEPHEN LANGTON

One writer called Stephen Langton "a personage of considerable historical importance whose thoughts and activities have a special interest." It is unfortunate that he must now be reintroduced to even students of history. He wrote the Magna Carta.

The date of Stephen's birth is unknown, but it is believed that he was born about 1165. He was from Lincolnshire, in northern England, probably of Anglo-Danish descent. His father was Henry Langton, a landholder on what was apparently a modest manor-- though the Langton's were able to provide an education for Stephen and his brother, Simon. Henry's third son Walter was apparently a wealthy man with high political connections, though upon his death he was found to be in debt to a well-known Jew from York. When Walter died, his wife remarried to Warin de Muntchenesy, whose first wife had been daughter to the famous knight William Marshal whom we will hear about later.

Stephen and Simon both entered the Catholic Church through their educational experience and made the decision to take holy orders. Their father Henry was not pleased with their choice to be clerics. None of the three sons left children to carry on the family name.

Stephen, the eldest son, probably received his early education from monks in the town of Lincoln, fifteen miles from their home in Wragby. Today that is considered but a short distance away, but in the late 12th century that fifteen miles would be perhaps a day's journey. It is believed that Stephen went to Paris about

30

the age of 15 in 1180 or so. The University in Paris was becoming a leading educational institution with a reputation of excellence in Theology though it was small with only about two hundred students. Universities of those days were like a combination high school and university today. Stephen (and later Simon) stayed at the university in Paris for his entire educational experience. Stephen did not leave until 1207, and by that time he was a faculty member with a reputation as a Theologian and Preacher having earned both Master and Doctor Degrees.

Some historians have suggested that the future Pope Innocent III, the most powerful pope of the century met and became friends with Stephen Langton while they were fellow students in Paris. Although the exact chronology of Langton's life is not well documented, it seems that a friendship is unlikely during their college years. It is true that in 1207, Innocent III summoned Stephen to Rome where he became a Cardinal, but Langton would have been a young student when Innocent left the university in 1185 about five years after Stephen arrived. Langton would have just completed his first degree when Innocent had graduated leaving his educational experience. It is more likely that as Langton's reputation grew during his twenty-five year career at Paris, Innocent learned of the other celebrated graduate from his own college. Innocent III was an active Pope who was always looking for dedicated talent for the Church, and he probably waited several years after Langton was a leader in Paris before the summons to Rome, not because they were "friends", but that Stephen's Paris ministry was working toward the very goals Innocent desired for the Church.

University education was a newly developing opportunity when Langton entered the institution. The curriculum was divided into *trivium* (grammar, rhetoric, logic), and *quadrivium* (arithmetic, music, geometry, astronomy). It would typically take a student about five years to complete the *trivium* and earn his baccalaureate degree. Then he could go on to complete the *quadrivium,* which could take an additional three or more years. It was possible to complete these courses in less time. All the courses were taught to prepare the student for service in the Catholic Church. There was only one church in Western Europe as the Protestant Reformation was about 300 years in the future--everyone was Catholic, heretic or pagan. The *trivium* was intended to make a student skilled in the use of Latin--the language of learning. Arithmetic was used to help train one to keep track of revenues and taxes, so this skill was also useful to those in government.

Geometry taught the transcendent truths of God and the universe as lines and angles interacted. Astronomy helped in predicting eclipses because the Church needed to have answers about these and other astronomical events to answer questions from peasant farmers and Princes alike. Music was training for use in church liturgy. The music of that day is now called Gregorian chant, named for Pope Gregory VII who ordered the Church to standardize its music. An authority on the history of church music describes Gregorian chant:

> "it consists of single-line melody sung to Latin words by unaccompanied men's voices in a flexible rhythm...in a scale different from our major or minor; it was impersonal, objective, other-worldly quality in which...beauty and emotion...are largely subordinate to expression of the religious content of the text."

This curriculum was based on traditional Roman methods as passed along through the medieval period of history, but change was in the wind. A hundred years later men known as "Scholastics" would seek to determine what truth was through the application of the logic taught by such Greek scholars as Aristotle.

Langton's education was not of this sort, but the idea was being discussed. The official position of the Catholic Church was that knowledge was the gift of God to man, and it was passed down authoritatively from generation to generation. If truth was logic based, then what becomes of the traditional authority of the Bible and the teachings of the Church? Since truth is absolute, there must be an absolute standard against which ideas must be tested. Stephen Langton chose to follow after the traditional methods, and he no doubt defended this course of thinking. Langton might best be understood as a leading intellectual of the end of the medieval educational system, not an early advocate of scholasticism. As we will see later however, Langton employed logic in his application of Theology and communication of his teachings (the "*Questiones*"), but he did not employ logic in the same way as a method of determining how truth is obtained. For Stephen Langton, truth is from the Bible, while application and interpretation come from the Pope with appropriate advice from theologians and other counselors.

Langton earned the equivalent of a Bachelor, Master, and Doctorate degrees, rising to the position of teacher while at the University of Paris. Teachers at Paris usually rented a room, and students paid for the privilege to hear the teachers' lectures. For convenience, the classes tended to be clustered in various sections of the city, though eventually, classes were held at the cathedrals of Paris. The famous Gothic style Notre Dame Cathedral was under construction (1163-1272) when Langton was living in Paris. In 1215, Pope Innocent III insured that the University in Paris would be established by confirming the organization of the institution. It was independent from local Church authorities, but instead it was organized as a self-governing corporation of teachers and students. Students lived under canon law (the law of the Church), not civil law. This gave students a certain protection from city authorities, a protection they tended to abuse.

The moral climate was supposed to be promoted by this legal standing, but in reality students were often unruly, in part because of this legal distinction. By 1215 when the University was officially recognized by the Pope, Stephen was no longer living in Paris, and he was occupied with other things.

While teaching at the University, Stephen was on the faculty of the school of Theology. In 1207 (the year Langton went to Rome) Pope Innocent III ordered that the number of Masters teaching Theology in Paris should be limited to eight to avoid confusion. Stephen was also busy writing commentaries on each of the books of the Bible and delivering sermons. We will look at his accomplishments in these areas in more detail later. Also Langton was a leader in redacting (putting in suitable form) the Latin Vulgate. While involved with this redaction project, Stephen Langton initiated some changes that affect all Christians down to the present day--he divided the books of the Bible into chapters. He also rearranged the order of some of the books of the Bible to place certain books near each other by subject (Gospels, History, Epistles, and Prophecy). His system of book arrangements did not become popular.

The Vulgate is a translation of the Bible from the original languages into Latin. This translation was made with the consent of the Pope by Jerome (347-420). It was thought necessary because educated people did not know Hebrew, Greek or Aramaic--the three languages in which the Bible was originally written. About three hundred years after Christ, the Jews translated their scriptures Christians call the Old Testament from Hebrew into Greek. Their translation is called the Septuagint as seventy scholars worked on this translation. The Septuagint set a precedent that it was acceptable for the Holy Scriptures to be written in a newer, understandable language in order that people could read and understand it. Jerome consulted the Septuagint while translating the Vulgate version of the Bible. "Vulgate" means "common" as in the common language. By Jerome's day the language of the Roman Empire and the language of learning was Latin, not Greek as it had been during the lifetime of the Apostles. Jerome's translation was intended to aid the Church in understanding the Bible better and to make it more accessible to the Christians of Europe. Like the Jewish translators, Jerome decided upon a translation procedure that did not translate word for word, but instead translated the meanings and phrases so it made sense in Latin. At the Tower of Babel God "confounded" the languages of man. Grammar, syntax, and of course vocabulary were mixed up in such a way that easy substitution of vocabulary was inadequate in the translation process. Jerome's procedure was the correct one as translators today would readily attest. This method, however, makes it necessary for the translator to make decisions about the intended meaning of the original document. This helps explain why there are several versions of the Bible today--

various theologies disagree on some of those choices about meaning when translating.

By Stephen Langton's day there was a problem with the Vulgate, but it did not relate to the issue of choices made by the translator. The problem was how copies were made. It would be another 150 years or so before Gutenberg would invent moveable type so the printing press could economically produce multiple copies of a book. Before Gutenberg books were hand copied one by one, and a book the size of the Bible could take years to produce. Copyists had different levels of skill. Some were more careful than others, some were even illiterate themselves so they simply copied the shapes they saw on the page. Over the nearly 1,000 years that had passed between Jerome and Langton there were errors in nearly every individual copy of the Bible available to the scholars in Paris. This lack of precision and uniformity must have been very frustrating to the Theologians at the University most famous for safeguarding the doctrines of the Catholic Church.

The Vulgate had been corrupted over time because of copying mistakes. Some passages had been omitted by accident. Some copies had misspellings. There were even additions made for the purpose of explaining or making a passage more clear--at least in the copyists' opinion. Langton began the process of redacting the Vulgate to correct these problems. He probably had assistance from others at the University--faculty and students who compared copies and made corrections. I imagine that in this process as an aid in keeping a group of readers together, Langton divided each book of the Bible into chapters. These chapter divisions were not made haphazardly as they demonstrate an understanding of the whole Bible. Of course two books of the Bible were divided into chapters right from the day

they were written: Psalms and Proverbs. Stephen Langton came to the study and exposition of the Bible as a teacher would, creating chapter divisions that had inner unity in thought and content. Most who read the Bible today tend to stop and start with these chapter divisions. Stephen Langton's chapter divisions were accepted by others of his time, and as a whole they have been accepted ever since. The "Paris Vulgate" was completed in 1227, but by then Langton was no longer living in Paris. Others completed the project in his absence but followed the pattern he established. When a version of the Vulgate was chosen for printing by Gutenberg, this "Paris Vulgate" with its chapter divisions was the one chosen. Protestants and Jews alike also use the same divisions. To be sure, there are criticisms of some of the choices Langton made. For instance Isaiah chapter 10 should have begun with verse 5 because those first four verses continue the judgment of Israel, and chapter 10 decrees judgment on Assyria.
 But such examples are pretty rare. Langton did NOT divide the Bible into verses--that was the work of Robert Estienne who devised our current system of verse divisions for a Greek New Testament in 1551 and for a French Bible in 1553. Verse divisions were made for publication on a printing press. The first English Bible with both chapter and verse divisions was the 1599 Geneva Bible, favorite of the English Pilgrims who came to America. After the Geneva Bible, nearly all Bibles were printed with chapter and verse divisions. Stephen Langton's contributions to the modern Bible alone should have established his reputation and name in Christianity and Western Civilization. Amazingly, however, Langton remains largely unknown.

   While in Paris, teaching at the University there, Stephen preached in various area churches and for various special occasions. For example, Stephen preached the funeral message of the "greatest knight in Europe", William the Marshal, when Langton was Archbishop of Canterbury. The teacher who had the greatest impact on Langton as a student was Robert de Courcon, a man with a wide reputation before Stephen enrolled at the University. Another significant person for both Langton and Courcon was a simple village priest named Fulk. This priest realized he needed additional education in order to properly fulfill his duties in a village near Paris, so he enrolled at the University. As his knowledge and confidence grew, Fulk began to preach more boldly and in a style consistent with his small-town church ministry. His style was humble and refreshing as well as practical for the regular daily life of a peasant. His sermons were not in Latin but in the common language of the people. As a result of Fulk's preaching a spiritual renewal swept through Paris in both the University and Cathedrals. Among those who were influenced by Fulk were Robert de Courcon and Stephen Langton. The existing sermons we have from Langton reflect the humility, simplicity and practicality of the humble village priest, Fulk. In one of his sermons, Langton said:

> "Christian men should not tempt God and start out, headlong and proudly, few against many, because they have a good Lord and a mighty. For God wishes His servants so to trust in Him that they be not reckless and neglect to work wisely."

Here we sense Langton's pious and sensible practicality. As for Courcon, Langton's teacher was known as one who spoke out against the cost and opulence of the Notre Dame Cathedral which was being constructed while they lived in Paris. Poverty and humility were very highly valued character traits in clergy, traits that the common Christian tended not to see in their educated spiritual leaders.

Langton's primary occupation was as a teacher of Theology at the University of Paris. He was very popular, and it was natural that his lectures would be put down in writing, and that these books would become valuable resources for his students, and even those who were not his students. In those days before the printing press, books were made by hand, so Stephen Langton's books were also copied by hand. It is assumed that all his books do not still exist today, yet the fact that any do, speaks to the enduring value of his writings. Since his teaching was considered expository (explaining the meaning of a passage of Scriptures in a methodical way), his writings are basically commentaries on the books of the Bible. Several of these commentaries still exist, and scholars have recently begun to study them.

ARCHBISHOP STEPHEN LANGTON

Chapter 4

THUNDERING TONGUE

As a Master at the University of Paris, Langton was expected not only to teach his students in the classroom but also to be an example to them of what a Godly clergyman should be. Part of that example was that he should preach, and Langton was a very significant preacher. He earned the nickname "Stephen of the Thundering Tongue" because of the power of his preaching and the way in which he preached.

Pope Innocent III was very much interested in things that would strengthen the Church and cause the people of Europe to live a truly Christian life. Langton was a part of that same group of concerned clergy. They were known as the Evangelical Movement or the *vita apostolica* movement. All the prominent preachers of this period of history were identified with this movement. The targets of concern included the clergy themselves, as leaders of the Church, and also the laity, or common, non-clergy people. Pope Innocent and many of the preachers were known for preaching to the clergy.

Langton also occasionally preached to the clergy, and of course he was training future clergymen, but his greatest emphasis was to preach to the laymen. The main message was for the hearers (both lay and clergy) to live a pure, Godly life. The Evangelicals preached against worldly wealth, greed and pride and they pled for a sincere prayer life and confessions for sins committed.

Stephen Langton's sermons that we have today (over 300 of them) are all written in Latin even though he often preached in the common tongue. His sermons were copied down by some person who was listening to the preaching, as was the practice at the University during classes. Since most common people did not know Latin, it was certainly students who recorded these sermons. The fact that the sermons we have were delivered in the Paris area during Stephen's time there, where there were plenty of students available for that task, explains the origin of these sermons. Later, perhaps many years later, the sermons were gathered together into collections which were then available for others to consult for sermon ideas and illustrations. The sermons of the great preachers of the day became sort of textbooks for other preachers to use in part or in whole. This same process was at work to create Stephen's commentaries.

Langton preached most often in the language of the people not Latin. By this period in history Latin was no longer used by the majority of the population. Regional languages were in the process of developing as various ethnic groups mixed together because of migration, invasion or even trade. In the Paris area people spoke in what we call today Old French. It was a combination of Celtic, Latin, various Germanic tongues spoken by the invaders who destroyed the Roman Empire, plus an influence from Scandinavia, brought to France by the Norsemen, many of whom settled from Normandy. In 1066 the Normans invaded England, so this Old French was also spoken in England during the reigns of the Norman kings. When Stephen went to England to be the Archbishop of Canterbury, the English were increasingly speaking what we call Middle English which was also a combination of various languages. Nearly two hundred years later Geoffrey Chaucer wrote *The Canterbury Tales* in Middle English, but that form of the language was far better developed than the language spoken in Langton's time. So Langton was at least tri-lingual. He was raised in England, so he knew Middle English, he studied in Paris, learning Old French, and the language of learning and of the Church was Latin. With all the confusion of languages in Europe, it made sense for the Church to use Latin in an attempt to unify the very linguistically confusing regions of the continent and to promote communication within the Church. Langton spoke and preached in all three of these languages. Very likely, he wrote only in Latin.

   The preachers of the Evangelical Movement did not challenge the doctrines of the established Church. However for Langton, obedience to the Pope was always couched in very specific terms. We will see this clearly when we discuss the Magna Carta story in detail, but it seems as though Stephen was very conscious of the human side of the Papacy, even while understanding that the Pope was God's spokesman on earth. Langton preached that Christ was the head of the Church, quoting Scripture (Eph. 4:15, Col. 1:17-18).
 Stephen Langton's first biographer (Matthew Paris) "found Langton a spokesman and representative of national feeling against Rome" in the context of England at the time of Magna Carta. This may be an overstatement of Stephen's attitude during the majority of his life. The preaching of Langton and others in the Evangelical Movement led to the establishment of the various Mendicant orders of preaching friars like the Benedictines whom Innocent III blessed at the Lateran Council of 1215. Friars of these monastic orders lived

and preached among the common people unlike the orders of cloistered (separated) monks. Preaching to the laity was not a new concept nor did it begin with the Evangelicals. Charlemagne was crowned Holy Roman Emperor in 800, and among his decrees is an order that preaching in the "language that the people would best understand" would be practiced in his empire. The problem in Charlemagne's day was that there were few clergymen with an education, and that problem had not been solved until the availability of schools was increased. The University of Paris was on the ground floor of that trend. Scripture asks "how shall they believe in him of whom they have not heard? And how shall they hear without a preacher?" (Rom. 10:14).

During Stephen Langton's lifetime which was at the end of the 12th and beginning of the 13th century, sermons were a bit more interactive than they usually are today. It was common for listeners (lay or cleric) to ask a question or to challenge the preacher on some point right during the preaching. A preacher had to be prepared to answer such interruptions. Langton wrote:

> "...a preacher should not always use polished, subtle preaching like Aod's sword, but sometimes a ploughshare, that is, a rude rustic exhortation. Very often a popular story...is more effective than a polished subtle phrase. Aod killed one man only with a two edged sword, Samgar six hundred with a ploughshare; so whereas the laity are easily converted by rude, unpolished preaching, a sermon to clerks will draw scarcely one of them from his error"

Aod (Ehud) and Samgar (Shamgar) are references to men from the book of Judges, and Stephen was using them as examples to illustrate his point. This was a common practice in 12th century preaching. The preachers of that day used scripture, allegory, satire, and rhymes in their preaching to make their messages memorable as lay audiences would not be writing down notes. Most people then were accustomed to remembering what they heard more so than today because of the necessity of knowing instructions and admonitions without being able to write things down for future reference. Langton also said about preaching:

> "Every preacher ought to have three things; he ought to think in advance about what he should say; he ought to pray to God that what he says is useful for himself and his listeners; he ought to live a good life, so that what he says by word is fulfilled by the example of good deeds."

Stephen's point about the preacher's life was a key part of his life message. Langton was known for his humility and purity of life.

Sermons of these times had a particular order for each service, much as we normally follow a particular order of service today. The first thing that was done in a service was the reading of Scripture. This was to show that truth comes from God in his revealed word. The preacher would announce the topic for the sermon (usually in Latin), then there would be an invitation to pray in which the preacher would humbly express his unworthiness to address the topic of the day. After prayer there would be a restatement of the topic (often in the common tongue), then the development of the sermon. Langton was known as an expository preacher. This meant that his goal was to explain the Scripture passage to his audience so they would both understand what it meant, and they would be motivated to live according to the teaching.

In the explanation Langton would use similes, metaphors, allegories and stories to explain the meanings and to teach the moral to his audience. Sometimes preachers used citations from other preachers, folk tales or from classical events or stories to illustrate what they wanted to preach. Stephen most often used the Bible itself to illustrate his points. These illustrative techniques were called *exempla*, and the University of Paris theology department was a major reason why the period from 1190 to 1225 was known as the "golden age of *exempla*" in Western Europe. Stephen Langton was a significant person in the creation of that reputation. The *exempla* often appeared toward the end of the sermon. Prayer ended the sermon portion of the worship service. The use of *exempla* marked a significant break from the Feudalistic mind-set of the previous era in which allegories were emphasized. During this same period there were major changes being made in painting, poetry and architecture as well.

In music Paris was a center for the development of the new polyphonic music. Notre Dame Organum was being composed by Leonin and Perotin during Langton's residence in the city. Polyphonic music had musical instruments and two lines of melody that moved independently of one another. Architecture also changed from the Romanesque style to the Gothic style: from round, heavy, solid appearance to the new pointed, airy, glass filled style. Notre Dame Cathedral is a prime example of the Gothic style. (The reader is encouraged to listen to samples of Gregorian Chant and polyphony from online sources).

In the 12th century there was a heavy use of allegory in preaching, but in the 13th century more exegesis was characteristic. Stephen Langton stood in the transition from one practice to the other. Exegesis, or explaining the meaning of the words and meaning of a passage of the Bible, required a great understanding of the entire Bible. Most preachers did not have that depth of knowledge, so they often consulted commentaries. The commentary would explain the meanings of key words found in the original Hebrew or Greek text, and they pointed out parallel passages in Scripture as well as explaining the meanings and applications of certain difficult to understand sections. The commentaries were the products of intense study, and Stephen Langton was a writer of commentaries. He is said to have written commentaries on every book of the Bible though we do not have all those commentaries today. Today scholars note that Langton's commentaries might be described as "medieval bestsellers" due to their popularity.

Judging from his own sermons, the Old Testament books that seem to be his special favorites were Ezekiel, Jeremiah and Isaiah. Among Minor Prophets, he frequently preached from Joel, Zechariah and Malachi. However, like other preachers of the period, he also often spoke from Job, Psalms, Proverbs and Ecclesiastes. From the New Testament, his most frequently used texts were the Gospels (Matthew, Mark, Luke and John), and the letters of St. Paul. Unlike contemporary preachers of the time, he seldom referred to secular writers.

In the education that Stephen received at Paris logic was taught before theology. This meant that the logic of Aristotle was seen as the basis of thought including theology. Langton was influenced by that progression. This expressed itself by him purposefully seeking to make the right argument to the right audience. He did not however, use logic to determine the nature of truth. He had total faith in the truth of Scripture even if the logic of the teaching seemed to be wrong from a human perspective. For instance he did believe in miracles though they are by definition illogical.

Langton allowed three divisions in explaining the sense of a passage of Scripture: the literal sense, the allegorical sense and the moral sense. To illustrate, a sermon by another preacher (Gilbert de Nogaret) presents a simple *exempla.* The word "Jerusalem" is explained literally by saying that there is an actual city named Jerusalem in the Holy Land. Allegorically, Jerusalem represents the Church. Morally, Jerusalem signifies a faithful person seeking eternal peace, which is obtainable by being obedient to the teachings of the Church.

Stephen preached against worldly wealth and greed. He held up the ideal of renouncing the things of this world and the importance of giving alms and doing good works, prayer, confessions, and penitence. Greed was presented as a sin of the clergy particularly those at higher levels of authority because this was the target of reform in the Evangelical Movement, and the general populace could readily see the abuses there. However Stephen also pointed out that one need not be wealthy to be greedy. He divided men into four groups on this topic: Those that have wealth and love it, those that have wealth and do not love it, those that have no wealth and do not love wealth, and those who have no wealth but they do love wealth. He noted that the last group was the most unhappy, and the happiest were the poor who were content. He frequently held up for an example the Godly man who resists the Devil by resisting greed, pride and lust. Langton's preaching was practical and realistic.

In one sermon he calls a merchant who brings to market an item that is plentiful "unwise". He says that it is wiser to sell things that are somewhat scarce, but in all transactions the merchant must deal honestly. He admonished partners to share in losses not just in the profitable times. The Church declared usury to be evil. They thought that it was immoral for one person to charge interest to someone who borrows taking the teaching of scripture (Ex. 22:25) as a command from God, not a principle for the nation of Israel. Langton taught against usury declaring it a great evil similar to adultery in that both are violations of God's law, and violations against ones neighbor thus doubly evil. In another sermon Stephen compares life to a ship--the prow and stern are narrow like life at the start and end, but the keel and middle of life are broad so as to bear the burdens of living. We see from these examples the practicality and memorable phraseology of Stephen Langton's sermon *exempla*.

More than the illustrations of the sermons Langton emphasized the vital importance of the preacher as the best example of Godliness. When speaking to clergymen he spoke boldly against the vices they were known for: greed, pride, purchasing appointments for the sake of making more wealth, keeping mistresses even after taking the vow of celibacy. Perhaps Langton earned his "Thundering Tongue" nickname while in the presence of this type of audience. To Stephen the clergy had important duties to perform for the vital spiritual health of Christians. It was their duty to God and the Church to live pure lives "least the lay folk try to excuse themselves by their ignorance because they do not understand scripture or because they are without preachers, whatever is contained in the holy church is displayed before them instead of a book...the laity should have those letters by which they can know God, and above all, ought to love and praise" (Him).

Here Langton was not calling for the Bible to be in the hands of laymen like the Protestant Reformation would three hundred years in the future. He was reminding the clergy that they were the "bible" that common men read, and they must present truth faithfully. Langton did not mention the Pope in his sermons. Because the Pope was head of the Church, this might be interpreted as disapproval of the great wealth the Pope held. On the other hand a prayer for the Pope was included in the order of service each time the congregation met so special further mention of the Pope might have been considered by him to be unnecessary.

In light of the fact that these sermons we still have were delivered during Stephen Langton's Paris years, and that he would eventually become involved in the politics of England when the Magna Carta was written, it would be good to consider what Stephen's views on government were, based on his sermons. As a member of the Evangelical Movement which taught that the Church was the vehicle for positive change in society he taught that the secular government must submit to divine lordship--lordship in the feudal obligation sense.

The king must be under the authority of God and His representative on earth was the Pope. This was called natural law, the law of creation. Kings were anointed by a high Church official like a Pope. According to Langton

51

the king was anointed to the service of the church, not to the ministry of God. Romans 13: 4 is often translated to read that the ruler is a "minister" of God, but it can also be rendered "servant" of God. The Church did not wish to elevate any king to the level of clergy in light of the fact that kings regularly conducted wars, and they did not take the vows a clergyman did. The inconsistency laid in the fact that while kings were not to be seen as clergy the Pope and many other clergymen were considered to be secular rulers over significant expanses of land and even contributed money and men for the conduct of war. If Langton recognized that inconsistency he never directly addressed it. He did often preach about justice that he defined as when "man returns to each man that which is his." He also taught that piety tempers justice by expressing compassion to paupers, and voluntarily distributing one's goods to the poor. Kings must be subject to natural law, but can act according to "custom" in his country as long as the two do not contradict each other.

    A person is not true king unless he is servant of God, and as an *exempla* Langton cited the King of England William Rufus, who was known as an evil person disobedient to God. Those under the king must obey the king as the king serves God. The Feudal system was built upon promises made between people, and the Church supported the concept of fulfilling one's promises. These issues would come into play later as Pope Innocent III became feudal lord over England and removed Langton from his Archbishopric for political not religious reasons. In that case, Langton refused obedience to the Pope on the grounds that he had made the decision based on incomplete information or insufficient council. These principles being discussed in theoretical terms during his Paris years would become very personal for Langton when he was an Archbishop in England.

Today we might wonder if Langton was (in Protestant terms) a "born again" man. Judging the faith of another is usually a useless activity as one cannot see the heart but only the outward behavior of another. Undoubtedly Stephen was a man of shining character fully dedicated to serving God as boldly and clearly as he was able. He was incredibly knowledgeable about the Bible and he tried to act out its teachings to the very best of his abilities. We cannot fault him for not expressing his faith in the terms used by Protestant Christians in Martin Luther's day three hundred years later, or even of John Wycliffe's time over a hundred years later. Stephen was a man of his time, a loyal Roman Catholic who went to confession, venerated Mary as "Mother of God", and believed in transubstantiation which is a doctrine that attributes a miracle during the mass where the bread and wine become the literal body and blood of Christ (Lk. 22:19-20). Transubstantiation and verbal confession to a priest were not official Catholic doctrines until 1215, the same year that Stephen was working on the Magna Carta. However Langton regarded these doctrines as issues of interpretation of Scripture within the responsibility of the Pope. He willingly submitted to Innocent's decisions about them. Some historians have suggested that Langton was an "Anglican before his time". This author recalls Heb. 11: 6 which assures us that "without faith it is impossible to please (God); for he that cometh to God must believe that he is, and that he is a rewarder of them that diligently seek him" (KJV).

Catholics might consider Stephen Langton a candidate for Sainthood. Protestants might consider him a medieval Catholic true believer. Since we cannot see his heart, only God knows his eternal destiny.

Stephen Langton is considered a "very important popular preacher of the late 12th century". "His reliance on scripture...shows him to be not only a traditional preacher...but also an important teacher of his students and his flock". Langton's "energies were directed toward the restoring of Christian teaching in all levels of society". For these reasons, Langton should have earned a prominent position in the historical memory of Christians in the Western Hemisphere.

Chapter 5

...AND A SCHOLAR

During his lifetime it was said of Stephen Langton that he was "a theologian known above all others of his time, who wrote many theological commentaries and books worthy of the consideration of later generations". Today there are about 120 manuscripts containing commentaries on the Bible he authored. Commentaries are commonly used today by students of the Bible to explain difficult passages, to assist in the preparation of sermons or to gather insights that a great scholar of the past might bring out to assist in a deeper understanding. During medieval times commentaries had the very same function. Preachers then may have used commentaries to a greater degree because there were fewer copies of the Bible, and because the commentaries were of shorter length, there were more of them. The commentaries sort of "digested" the Scriptures for a preacher, allowing him to know less himself, but instead to depend on the scholarship of another. As we have seen, Langton's sermons were popular as a guide for less trained preachers of his era. Stephen's commentaries were another aid for these same preachers.

   We are confident that Langton wrote a commentary on every book of the Bible including the apocrypha. The apocrypha are religious writings of very old age that have been included with the Bible, but have traditionally never been accepted as inspired like the other books of the Bible. It is not within the scope of this biography to describe how books of the Bible are inspired or not, but it is important to know that the inspired books have been accepted by Christians as messages from God Himself written by human authors who were "moved by the Holy Spirit" (2 Pet. 1:21) to write those messages down for the education and encouragement of future generations. The apocryphal books were included in all Bibles until the 1885 edition of the King James Bible, and they were read as stories with historical value, but Christian doctrine was not based on anything contained in these extra books. Stephen Langton did write commentaries on the apocrypha, as did other commentators. Perhaps because of this practice, the Catholic Church began to gradually use the apocrypha as the basis for doctrines which is another distinction between Catholicism and Protestantism.

Many of Langton's commentaries exist today in three forms. Just as sermons of this period of history included a "literal" explanation of Scripture, then a "moral" explanation, these two types of commentaries are available. Langton's commentaries are also available as combination, or "full" commentaries. Historians who have studied this situation agree that the "full type" was produced first, and then the other types were created later. This would make the commentaries more quickly available (thus less expensive), and it would provide a more specialized assistance to the preachers. The commentaries were produced during Stephen's years in Paris, about 1180 to 1206, so over the centuries there are commentaries that exist in partial form, but not full or full and not partial. At any rate, the fact that so much effort was extended to produce these commentaries and the fact that the manuscripts are spread over most of Europe indicates that Langton's commentaries were in high demand over an extended period of time.

Evidence exists that many of these commentaries were copied down as Stephen taught them in his classes as students recorded them. Then Stephen might read these over making comments or corrections before more copies were made. So the commentaries tell us as much about his teaching ministry as it does about his writing. All of Langton's commentaries are written in Latin, the language of the Church, the language he used when teaching. Commentaries in Old French would have been of limited use, and would have required translation. The commentaries begin with Genesis and progress over time through the New Testament, apparently in the order the books of the Bible are found in our Scriptures today.

The content of the commentaries is very much like the sermons he preached in content and approach. There is a heavy dependence on the words of Scripture itself with careful consideration of context. The commentaries show an effort to make the understanding clear by the use of illustrations, many of which are from the life experiences of the people he is targeting--the students at the University of Paris. Certain "current event" references are made by way of illustration such as the Crusades. From Judges 3:15 Stephen said that King Eglon represents greed and those that send him gifts by the hand of their leader remind Langton "of those who serve the church with an eye to their own profit." His commentary on the book of Genesis addresses the question "was the moon created full?" since the heavenly bodies was created on day four of creation. Because of the medieval emphasis on and belief in the significance of numbers, the popular belief was that the moon was in its tenth day phase "in eternity", so creation would begin on phase day eleven, and the moon would have been created on its phase

58

day fourteen. Langton assured in his commentary that the moon was created in full phase day one dismissing popular belief.

Besides the commentaries Stephen Langton also wrote poetry. It is recorded that he wrote a series of poems dedicated to the Virgin Mary. It is also known that he wrote a biography of King Richard the Lionhearted. Neither of these works remains today. Richard had spent much of his time as King on crusade. This was a popular thing to do among the general populace and within the Church. The purpose of the Crusades was to free the Holy Land from the grip of the Muslims. By the time of the Third Crusade, the one that Richard led, the city of Jerusalem had fallen to Muslim control again.

Chapter 6

KING JOHN AND ELEANOR

If there had not been a King John, there would not have been a Magna Carta. John was such a bad king, he was considered to be a serious threat to the very existence of England as a free nation. Back when the hated William Rufus was king, he was assassinated, and nobody mourned his passing. A similar solution was also possible when it came to John, but because of the previous history England had experienced, and because of the wise leadership of Stephen Langton, the Barons of the nation first tried the solution of written law to restrict and redirect the course of England achieving the happy result of peace and stability. Assassination would have certainly contributed to civil war and prolonged the invasion from France. Langton stepped up to be the leader England needed in this serious crisis that was brought on by one evil, selfish and inept man, King John Softsword.

    Upon the death of Henry I (1135) there was a war of succession, usually called the Anarchy, between Matilda (daughter of Henry I and Matilda of Scotland) and Stephen, (son of Henry I's sister Adela and Stephen Blois). Henry I's daughter Matilda was married to Geoffrey of Anjou, usually called Plantagenet because he wore a sprig of broom plant in his hat. This period of Anarchy divided the loyalties of the barons of England and Normandy. Stephen was not a wise leader nor was he bold so as a result, he did not attract support. Matilda's husband was a descendent of Fulk III "the Black" who, according to tradition had made a league with the Devil. The family was known for violent fits of anger at fairly unpredictable times. Geoffrey Plantagenet carried that same reputation for uncontrolled violence and rage, so the barons were not attracted to that side of the conflict either. As each side burned and pillaged villages, razed castles, and generally caused great suffering across the kingdom, people of all classes longed for peace. It was finally agreed that Matilda's son, Henry would become King Henry II of England, and Duke of Normandy. Literally days before Geoffrey Plantagenet died Henry married Eleanor of Aquitaine. Henry was 18 years old Eleanor was 28. Only two months prior she had been Queen of France.

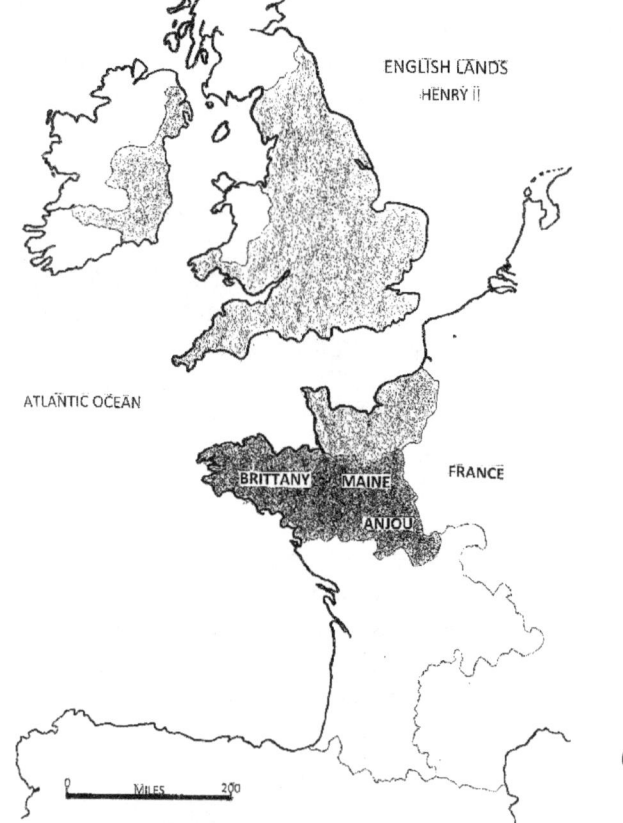

Eleanor was renowned for her beauty, and as the daughter of the Duke of Aquitaine, a very rich holding in southern France. She was well educated both formally and practically in the affairs of state as her father's heir. She had been married to Louis, Prince of France as a political alliance, when she was 15 years old. Within days of the wedding the King of France died so Louis became King Louis VII and she, his Queen. Louis would have rather been a clergyman, and the tedium of ruling was not his passion although it was for Eleanor. She recognized this immediately and loved to dominate his decisions and policies. Competing for Louis' ear was Abbot Suger who had very different advice for the King. Eleanor's advice led to several unproductive wars in the south of France, but Louis was so in love with his beautiful wife it took some time for him to realize that she was the reason for his frustration in politics and war. Eventually he followed Suger's advice, and his own inclination, and decided to take up the cross and go on Crusade. Eleanor decided to go with him taking along with her a number of other noblewomen. The wagons carrying their comforts slowed the army considerably. The King and Queen eventually made it to Constantinople where true luxury was demonstrated to Eleanor, and she loved it. Later when they got to Antioch they were treated well by the European ruler there, Eleanor's cousin. Militarily speaking little was accomplished on this crusade. The journey to and from the Holy Land was an ordeal in itself, and the two years it took was a sacrifice and a huge financial drain on the people of France. While in Antioch Louis and Eleanor had a loud and public argument in which hurtful things were said on both sides. The division between them was significant, and even the kindly intervention of the

Pope himself as they journeyed through Italy on the return trip, was not sufficient to heal the breach. After returning from the Crusade Eleanor suggested that their marriage be annulled. Though she had given birth to two girls Louis still did not have the son he so much desired to carry the family into the next generation as King. According to the complicated rules used by the church to determine if the couple was too close in ancestry to be legally married, Louis and Eleanor qualified for an annulment even after thirteen years of marriage. So the Pope declared them no longer husband and wife.

    Eleanor returned to her Duchy in Aquitaine but the leading men there were not happy and one of them tried to kill her in an ambush. Another tried to capture her to force her to marry him. By riding hard in disguise she was able to escape to a "safe" fortress, but it was obvious that she needed a militarily powerful husband to even rule her own inheritance. Two months after the annulment Eleanor had negotiated a marriage performed in December 1154 to Henry Plantagenet, son of Geoffrey. Henry was ten years younger than herself but the political potential was huge. Henry was to be the Duke of Normandy and King of England. When Eleanor's land was added to Henry's, and additional land was acquired soon after their wedding they controlled all of western France, England, Wales, and had huge influence in Scotland. Eleanor was once again a Queen. She would give birth to five boys (Richard and John, later ruled England), and three girls who would be instrumental in solidifying alliances with other kingdoms.

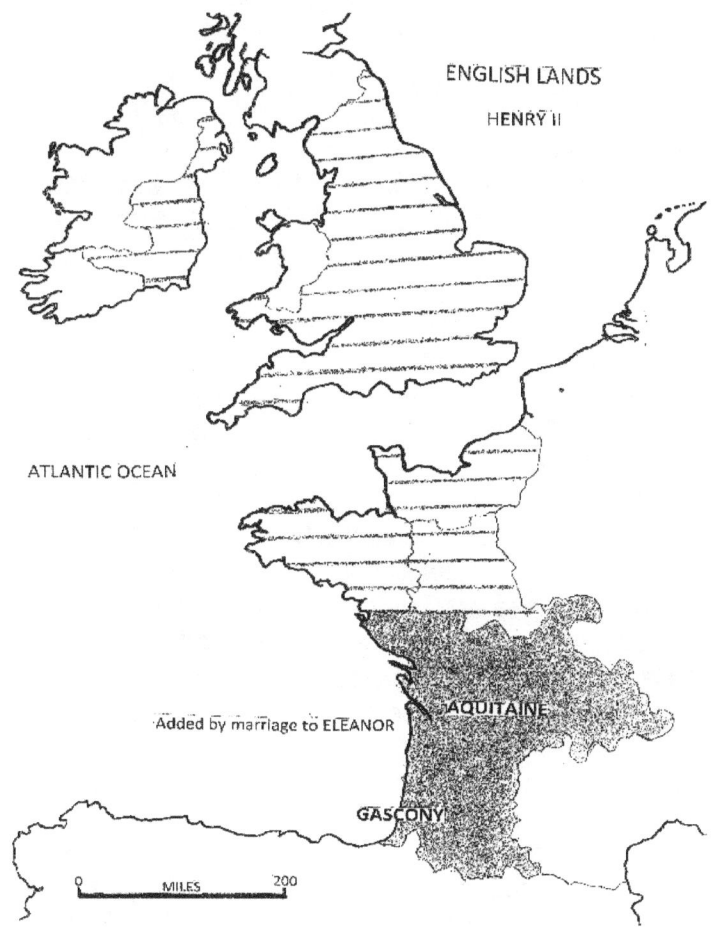

    Eleanor had married a man who was a good administrator and warrior. However, for some time she helped rule the domain issuing laws and commands in her own name, as well as in the name of King Henry II. She also brought the courtly culture of southern France to the court of England. Their son (another Henry) was engaged to marry the daughter of the king of France (as he had remarried also). King Louis VII had developed into a subtle negotiator, and even though it appeared that Henry II was the stronger monarch both he and

Eleanor owed feudal obligations to Louis, a fact that Louis used to his advantage.

As time went on and King Henry became more accomplished in his role he needed Eleanor less. She turned her attention to her three most promising sons (Henry, Richard and Geoffrey), exercising an influence over each of them to a far greater degree than King Henry understood or appreciated. Eleanor lived to be 80 years old, and up to the very end she was influencing events in Europe to a much greater degree than her role as Duchess of Aquitaine or Queen Mother warranted.

Part of the blindness that Henry had about his children was because of the troubles he was having with Thomas Becket. Becket served as Henry II's most trusted counselor. They seemed to think alike and Becket was a very energetic and gifted administrator. Becket seemed to anticipate the needs and desires of the King, and Henry certainly appreciated that. When the Archbishop of Canterbury died Henry saw an opportunity to gain control of the churches in England-- appoint Thomas Becket to that most powerful church position in the nation. First Becket had to take Holy orders and become ordained, but within a year this was accomplished, and he was now Archbishop Thomas.

From that moment, Thomas became a different man. Whereas before he totally enjoyed the wealth and luxury his position as King's counselor, now he gave away all his wealth. Instead of wearing fine clothes, he wore the habit of a monk, complete with hair shirt next to his skin. Thomas invited beggars to live in his home. He fasted and prayed several days a week. There were more new habits but most importantly to King Henry, Becket became as dedicated to the Church as he had previously been to the King. Thomas began to strongly defend the privileges and power of the Church from the power of the King. The old investiture issue again became a point of conflict between the King and the Archbishop. Henry could not understand the radical changes he saw in Thomas, and he was hurt and angered by what he viewed as betrayal. Becket saw his new position as a chance to prepare for eternity, and he took his church vows very seriously. Becket was ordered out of the country by Henry, and remained in exile for some years before a temporary reconciliation was arranged by friends. But peace between them was short lived.

Finally, in his frustration Henry expressed a desire that someone would rid him of this thorn in his side, and four of his knights took it upon themselves to act in a way they thought would please the king. They rode to Canterbury and found the Archbishop standing at the altar where they killed him before fleeing. When Henry heard the news he was horrified. He knew that his uncontrolled anger had created this unacceptable situation, but he did not really want to see Thomas dead, and especially murdered inside a church. Churches were seen as places of sanctuary, and violence was absolutely abhorrent. In a short time, miracles were attributed to the place where Thomas Becket was killed. Common people, clergy and foreign leaders were outraged with what had occurred. Henry wrote letters to the Pope denying any part in the murder of Becket. The murderers themselves were excommunicated by the Pope, along with any others "who may have assisted them". Within two years, the Church sainted Thomas, and Henry twice allowed himself to be publicly flogged as he prostrated himself before the church and public opinion. In reality, no ruler can do whatever he wants contrary to the people's willingness to endure (I Kings 12:6-16), and Henry painfully discovered that truth. This episode in Henry's life, this fall from the heights of power is part of the background that led to the Magna Carta. Henry was to suffer even more humiliation before his life ended.

Not long before this miscalculation regarding Becket, Henry chose another self-destructive course. He became involved with another woman, known as Fair Rosemound. This was not a brief encounter. If it had been, it could have been weathered, it could have been forgiven. Henry installed Fair Rosemound in one of his estates, and the arrangement was not kept secret. He seemed to be purposefully estranging himself from his wife without a care for anything but his own desires. Eleanor returned to her beloved Aquitaine where she strengthened her hold on her own lands, and developed strong relationships with her sons. She began to plan the long and stealthy plot to undermine her husband and install one of their sons as King, in her own mold.

The sight of King Henry being humiliated publicly was more than his sons could stand. The eldest son Henry had already been promised the kingship over England and Normandy, and he began to think that the present was a good time to make the transition from his discredited father to himself. His brothers Richard and Geoffrey supported his decision to rebel against Henry II because they too wanted to exercise actual authority over the domains they had been promised. The King seemed to be incapable of effectively resisting the rebellions and surrender of castles occurring all over the kingdom.

Each of the brothers turned to the king of France for protection and military assistance. There was significant disruption in the domains of Henry II as various barons shifted their allegiance from the King to one of his sons, to the French then back and forth again as the fortunes of war shifted. In the confusion of the time, Eleanor found it dangerous to travel, but that did not stop her from doing her part to negotiate alliances and to do what she could to weaken King Henry's stock on the continent. Finally, Eleanor was taken out of the equation when she was captured while traveling with a small group of her trusted knights while dressed as a man.

Henry then confined her in England and tried his best to isolate her from contacting her sons or anyone else.

Eleanor was 53 years old at the time of her capture. In 1176 Fair Rosamond died. Then in 1183, Henry the young king was stricken with a disease at age 28. Before he died, he sent a message to his father asking for forgiveness, and it was granted. Many in Europe mourned Henry's passing as he had the kind of personality that attracted love and support from the people.

Just three years later, Henry II died. This meant that in the midst of a rebellion there was no king. Eleanor, who was now 67 freed herself from captivity and began touring across England doing all she could to stir support for her son Richard to be the next king.

Geoffrey had also died by then, and the choice was between Richard and Geoffrey's son Arthur. But Arthur was a teenager, and he had seldom even visited England. As queen, Eleanor's support was vital. She also began to issue orders that would garner support for the change to a new king. She released prisoners where she traveled; she declared the establishment of uniform standards of weights and measures, and of coinage. By this time, the towns and cities were becoming increasingly financially important, and these measures were extremely popular with the businesses in those towns. So with the support of Eleanor, Richard was crowned king of England.

Richard, like his brother Henry, was tall, handsome, and very likeable. He would become one of the most popular kings in English history. It is said that Richard was "a passionate man...(who) did not shrink from any kind of debauchery...(but) he was capable of repenting as immoderately as he had sinned". As one of Richard's first acts as king, he declared that he was going on a crusade. This was a critical time in the Holy Land, as the Muslims had recaptured Jerusalem and the famous Saladin was unifying the entire region from Egypt to Turkey. Richard, Philip of France and Henry Barbarossa Holy Roman Emperor, all planned to respond to the need to recapture Jerusalem. This Third Crusade was known as the "crusade of kings" and potentially, it could have been as successful as the First Crusade. But it was not. Barbarossa died enroute while crossing a river. Richard offended Philip by his aggressive military achievements and Philip returned home with his army. So Richard carried on without the military support of the other two armies, eventually winning a treaty with Saladin that granted limited military and religious concessions. Richard did make for himself a great reputation as a warrior at the battles of Acre, Blanch-Garde, Ascalon and Jaffa. While Richard was not able to win back Jerusalem, he had seen success in helping to capture the port city of Acre, and had shown exceptional valor at risk of his own life when recapturing Jaffa. Jaffa had been taken after Richard had defeated a force led by the Muslim hero Saladin at Arsuf. As Richard was retreating from Jerusalem, Saladin attacked Jaffa, recapturing most of the city with an army of thousands. Richard rushed a small army to relieve his garrison in Jaffa, but when he arrived, found the city under control of the Muslim forces. However, Richard attacked the city from the sea, leading only 54 knights, a few hundred infantry and about 2,000 crossbowmen attached to the navy that had brought him. Probably wielding his favorite weapon, a broad axe, Richard's bold surprise attack carried the day, and his forces were able to retake the city. As a result of this victory, Saladin was willing to make an agreement with Richard that ended the Third Crusade and allowed limited Christian access to the Holy sites in Jerusalem.

Richard's personal bravery and bold tactics earned him the title "Lionhearted" and the affections of the English people. Back in England, William Longchamp ruled the country with a heavy hand that made the people long for the return of Richard. Eleanor also was active in governing, mostly in the French areas where her support was greatest. Eventually she was successful in deposing Longchamp, and she exiled him from England.

Eleanor also kept a sharp eye on her son John who was entirely unlike his brothers Henry and Richard. People believed "there was a devilish spirit in him", and their use of the word "devilish" was in a literal sense. "Oaths and promises meant nothing to John". Henry II had not promised any land for John to rule, in fact Henry himself called John "Lackland". John's father seems to have liked him, but apparently nobody else in the family did. He was deceitful and conniving. When Richard was captured and held for ransom in Germany as he was attempting to return to England, John once again began to maneuver to take the kingdom from the absent Richard. John wanted the crown and Richard had seemed to indicate that his nephew, Arthur of Brittany should rule if Richard did not return from the crusade.

Eleanor resisted John as much as she could. A massive ransom was demanded of England for the return of Richard, and Eleanor was the chief fund-raiser. Every freeman was required to contribute one quarter of his yearly income, churches were stripped of their treasures, and the Cistercian monks who lived in poverty were required to contribute their entire wool production (a very significant tax). In over a year of effort the 150,000 marks, equaling about 35 tons of silver, was raised. Eleanor now 72 years old, accompanied the treasure to Germany and received her son again.

    Richard was still popular in England even after being absent for four years, but on the continent, his military power was required to win back the authority his father had once enjoyed. John had been effective in undermining Richard. While engaged in winning back his authority on the continent, Richard was shot in the back by a crossbowman. The wound festered, and within a week Richard was dead at age 41, but not before he was reconciled with John. Eleanor now must work more diligently than ever to ensure that her last son would rule. In this endeavor, Eleanor had the assistance of an extraordinary man, who had been a part of the ruling structure of England for many years, the man Stephen Langton called "the greatest knight that ever lived", William Marshal.

WILLIAM MARSHAL

First Earl of Pembroke

CHAPTER 7

THE GREATEST KNIGHT

William Marshal's earliest memory was when he was about five years old. His father John FitzGilbert was in a castle being besieged by Stephen Belois during the Anarchy in 1152. FitzGilbert sent William to Stephen as a surety that a negotiated truce would not be broken. If FitzGilbert broke the truce, young William would be killed, but FitzGilbert did break the truce when he brought in reinforcements. Stephen was a kindly man and William was a cheerful, bold child. While in captivity, William played among the besiegers' tents and even enticed Stephen to play with him. William devised a game in which each person would hold a clump of flowers and "attack" the flowers held by the other. William succeeded in knocking off the heads of the flowers held by Stephen, thus winning the game. When Stephen saw that FitzGilbert had won an advantage by breaking the truce, he declared that he would kill the child if FitzGilbert did not return his defending army to its original numbers. FitzGilbert responded that there were more sons where this one came from. Stephen could not bring himself to actually kill William, and the fortunes of war turned such that within two years the war ended, and William was returned to his family.

William was born about 1146, the fourth son of the English baron FitzGilbert. Since the universal practice in England was that the eldest son received the greatest portion of his father's wealth, the fourth son had no prospect of receiving any significant wealth when his father died. So at age 13 William was sent to Normandy to live with his father's cousin, William of Tancarville who was a powerful baron. It was hoped that William would learn to be a knight and earn his existence in the service of such a lord as Tancarville, who had 94 knights in his household. Young William became a squire where he learned to care for horses, weapons and armor of the knights. He also learned the skills of a knight, and wore the chain-mail hauberk when the baron was at war. He also had to learn to live with the privations and rigors of knighthood. That life included religious devotion, or at least respect for religion. A knight and his squire were expected to treat women kindly, be generous to his fellows and the poor, and perhaps to learn the songs of troubadours who composed titillating songs of courtly love. William was known as a knight who could sing well. The most important lessons involved the ethics of knighthood.

William Marshal learned to be a powerful warrior who was absolutely truthful and loyal. These character traits marked his entire life. Then, on the eve of a war twenty one year old Squire William was officially knighted.

In 1167, about the time of Stephen Langton's birth, William was with his uncle and a few other knights who composed a security guard for Queen Eleanor of Aquitaine. The company was attacked by a superior number of knights. Tancarville sent Eleanor to escape with a few knights while he and his remaining force stood to resist the attack. Tancarville was killed.

William was unhorsed, but he backed up to a hedge and verbally taunted the attackers to come and get him.

Eventually one of his opponents attacked from behind him by leaping his horse through the hedge and stabbing William in the leg. William was captured, and he had to tend his own wound while traveling with his captors. Such wounds normally become infected and lead to death because people then knew little about cleaning a wound to avoid fatal infections. Eleanor had escaped, but not before seeing what Tancarville and the others were doing to shield her escape. In gratitude she ransomed William and brought him to her household. This was a significant change of fortune for William as it placed him on the track to fame and glory.

When William was 25, Eleanor entrusted him with mentoring her son Prince Henry, heir to the English throne. William would be companion to the "young king" Henry for the next 25 years. Henry was about ten years younger than William, and by this time Marshal was an accomplished and bold knight. Besides training Henry in the art of war, William was entrusted with all security arrangements for Henry. By 1180 William was made a baronet with a contingent of knights under his authority, but he owned no land. Meanwhile, Langton was just entering the University in Paris. Prince Henry had been promised that he would rule after his father, but he had not been given any actual authority or lands of his own to rule. When his father was experiencing troubles concerning the death of Thomas Becket, Prince Henry decided it was time this situation changed, so he rebelled against King Henry II. At that time William knighted the "young king" in the presence of the French princes and nobles. William's loyalty had been transferred from Tancarville to Eleanor and now to Henry. It is very likely that he now fought against King Henry in the rebellion.

Eventually the rebellion came to an end, and as a result the young king received two castles and the lands associated with them. In addition, he received 1,500 pounds annually from King Henry II in currency. This money could be cut off easily and thus felt more like an allowance than true income. The barons of the realm had many more castles than two, and these two were not strategically situated. At the age of 20 years, young Henry certainly was not happy with this settlement, but now he at least could properly equip a small contingent of knights to join him at the tournaments, and possibly build some independent wealth.

In 1176 Prince Henry and William Marshal were involved in several tournaments. The nature of tournaments changed as time went on, but in the later 12th century a tournament (or melee) was sponsored by kings or barons. The sponsor would announce when and where the contest would be held, often inviting certain renowned knights to attend. He might also suggest the makeup of each army, such as "French" against "Norman". Knights attended such tournaments in order to win some wealth. Men like William seldom had any land to financially support themselves. The purpose of the fighting was to capture their opponents. The knight, his armor and his horse, together or separately, could command a ransom for their return. Sometimes a knight might capture a horse he wished to keep for himself or to give to a friend. Occasionally a knight would be killed in battle, but that was not the intent. A dead knight earned no ransom. After a tournament, there would be a big banquet or several banquets. The sponsor might offer a banquet to recognize the best knights. A knight who was especially successful in getting captures might sponsor a banquet where he would entertain his captured foes, and perhaps the barons who might help pay their ransoms.

In the 12th century armor was not yet the solid, fully encasing barrier of metal that we often think of. That sort of armor would not develop for another 100-150 years after William. In his day armor was a hauberk of interlinked chain that extended from shoulder to knee with a slit between the legs so the knight could sit astride a horse. The legs were also covered in chain mail with the arms, hands, and feet also similarly covered. A coif covered the head, neck, shoulders, and upper chest and back. On his head would be a helmet most commonly made from strips of metal riveted together, often with two layers of metal. There may also be a strip of metal extending down the length of the nose to protect it. Another type of helmet reminds one of wearing a bucket on his head, with a slit, or slits for the eyes and holes to help the knight breathe. Shields were usually triangular in shape made from wood with a water hardened leather coating. It was lightweight and could be used as a weapon as well as a means to deflect blows from other weapons. The preferred weapon of a knight was usually a sword, but a mace (heavy ball on a stick) or battle-axe might be the choice of some. Lances were used to knock a knight off his horse. These weapons and the armor could be separated from the knight when ransom negotiations began.

    A knight's horse was also fair game for capture in a tournament. Any horse used for battle was called a destrier. A destrier was well trained for battle responding to spoken commands, knee pressure, as well as by bridle. They were strong, especially in the hindquarters, agile and fast. They were usually stallions as mares are naturally smaller. A destrier is not a breed of horse, but a well-trained horse of good size (14-16 hands tall at the shoulder). Destriers were highly desired, and comparatively rare and expensive. Saddles for such a horse looked different from the common saddles of today. The knight needed all the help he could get to stay on the horse, so the saddles offered wooden and leather "fences" both behind him and in front of him that were four to five inches high. The saddle was secured under the horse with two straps or girths. Stirrups had been invented in Asia many centuries before this, and were necessary for medieval battle in Europe. Nearly as expensive as a destrier was a palfrey. A palfrey may have been a breed of horse that was known for its gentle gait of front left, back left followed by front right, back right legs moving together. The gait is known as an amble. Most horses do not amble as their legs move in a left front, rear right leg motion. A palfrey could amble for long distances at a quick pace for a long time. Riders find the amble to be much more comfortable than any other gait. Often a knight would ride a palfrey for travel, and then transfer to his destrier when preparing for battle. Women also preferred palfreys. Another breed favored by women was a Jennet because they were quiet, gentle and smaller than other horses. Jennets were bred in Spain and used by the Spanish cavalry in conflicts against Muslims. A general purpose horse was a rouncy. These were less expensive and so were used by squires and other men-at-arms as well as by younger, less-wealthy knights. A rouncy could also be used as a pack horse. All horses had some value as income sources at a tournament.

After one particular tournament, William received acclaim as a leading knight of Europe. This special tournament was attended by the best knights from many domains and included important barons and princes, with their associated bodyguards and key knights. The wife of the tournament sponsor wished to give a prize to the best knight of the tournament--a spectacularly crafted and ornately decorated lance. At the post-tournament banquet, the lance was given to an important prince. He chivalrously declined it, and presented it to another, who declined and humbly passed it to another. Around the banquet several different knights were offered the lance, but none would accept the honor of being the best knight of the tournament as each could think of someone else who deserved it more. Finally, the assembled knights began to propose the names of the truly greatest and soon, William Marshal was acclaimed as the best--but he was absent from the banquet. A select committee was chosen to find William and to present the lance to him in the name of the great lady and the assembled knights.

After a few hours, the committee returned to report that Marshal had been found--in a blacksmith shop. He was found with his head on the anvil, with the blacksmith standing over him with hammer and tongs. The blacksmith was attempting to remove his helmet that had been so bashed and dented that William could not remove it. All present at the banquet were now assured that the lance had indeed been awarded to the greatest knight among them. In 1177--about the time Stephen Langton was earning his first degree in Paris--William Marshal and his friend Roger de Gaugi were entering as many tournaments as they could. In ten months, they captured 103 knights, plus other valuable booty.

In 1182 a rumor was circulating that Marshal was inappropriately associating with another man's wife. Marshal denied it, but the rumor would not die, so William separated himself from the young king and his responsibilities to Henry, and went out to earn his living from tournaments alone. Within a year, Prince Henry became ill and died. William was present when Henry was ill and promised to go on crusade on Henry's account. Marshal was gone for two years, and although no records remain about his exploits in the Holy Land, we can safely assume that he played the part of a Christian knight while battling Muslims.

Upon his return, we find him associated with King Henry II again. We know that William Marshal pleased the King because, although King Henry trusted his own son Henry very little and would not give him any significant lands, yet he promised William he would arrange a marriage between Marshal and the very wealthy Isabel de Clare. She was heir to a large portion of the Clare fortune that included extensive lands in the volatile and strategically important Wales, as well as lands in Ireland. This is the same Clare family that was so strongly implicated in the assassination of King William Rufus nearly two hundred years earlier. King Henry II died in 1189, but the wedding had not yet been performed. This was very important for William, who was now 42 years old and near the end of the career for most knights.

Before Henry fell ill, his sons rose in rebellion against him once again. Richard was the son most likely to follow in Henry's footsteps, but as a loyal knight of the king, William Marshal was fighting for Henry's cause against the man who would probably soon be king.

About a week before Henry died, Richard was in pursuit of his father when he met Marshal on the road. William could have killed the son of his sovereign, but Richard was unarmed and to kill an unarmed opponent would be a breach of the chivalric code, so William killed Richard's horse instead to slow his pursuit of the King.

Soon after, the newly crowned King Richard met with William and they discussed that incident and William's future. Richard was a wise and honorable man who understood that he could well use a loyal man such as William Marshal. So Marshal was forgiven, and the wedding to Isabel de Clare was approved.

Soon thereafter William Marshal was a rich and powerful baron, husband of a beautiful young wife (age 19) and in good standing with King Richard. William and Isabel were parents of two sons and three daughters. Right up until the end of William's life he and Isabel were tenderly romantic toward each other. William's new title was Earl of Pembroke. He was now among the largest land holders, one of the wealthiest barons in England. Much of his land was in Wales, an area that was only barely under the control of the king. William built the "keep", or central tower of a new Pembroke Castle, the ruins of which can still be visited, in Wales. The Welsh had been stubbornly independent ever since Roman days. The new Earl also owned land in Ireland, England and Normandy. Only the strongest and most trusted men were given authority in Wales and Ireland.

While Richard was in the Holy Land during the Third Crusade, William Marshal was occupied solidifying his rule in Ireland and Wales, succeeding in making the landholdings there more productive thus increasing his wealth. It was during this period that William began constructing the Keep at Pembroke. Richard made his journey home, but was captured in Austria, then sold to a German baron. It is thought that the French king contributed to the plot to keep Richard out of England. Richard's brother John was agitating to become the next king, and Eleanor was attempting to counter John's moves and keep hope in Richard alive. Finally, a ransom amount was demanded to return Richard to his home. Due to the efforts of the hated William Longchamp and the Queen Mother Eleanor, within 18 months the first installment of the ransom was paid, the hostages surrendered, and Richard returned to his throne. The damage done by John remained, so

Richard spent most of his time repossessing his lands in Normandy. It was then that Richard was shot in the back by a crossbowman. Richard lay dying as William Marshal and Archbishop of Canterbury Hubert Walter consulted with one another about who should reign next. Walter preferred Arthur of Brittany, Richard's nephew. Marshal preferred John, saying that John was English, and Arthur had seldom even visited England. Richard seemed to indicate that John follow him as king so it was settled. When John ascended to the throne, the lives of John, William Marshal and Stephen Langton became entwined, and the most significant result was the Magna Carta.

KING JOHN

Chapter 8

KING JOHN REIGNS

Throughout history there have been a few thoroughly evil characters--Adolph Hitler immediately comes to mind. Although there are some dissenters, most biographers of King John would put John in the same category as Hitler. Some of the comments about John include "there is nothing we can admire...there is nothing that we can pity", "foul as it is, Hell itself is defiled by the presence of King John". He is described as having "disgusting duplicity" of being "malevolently capricious", "almost superhumanly wicked". His vices include "merciless inhumanity", "licentious indulgence" and practicing "paralyzing extortion" on his own subjects. The hatred expressed toward this man has been pushed aside by a few historians as later justification for the humiliation imposed upon John in the form of the Magna Carta. However, the stories told, the verifiable events recorded and the breadth of negative feelings expressed, point very strongly toward believing the evil reports about him. His very depravity motivated the barons and the Archbishop to write and insist he be restrained by the Magna Carta

King Richard died in 1199. Soon thereafter John was crowned King of England and Duke of Normandy at the age of 32. He was a bit shorter than his brothers, standing about 5'6" tall, and he had a darker complexion like his southern French ancestors. His mother Eleanor was 75, and she had the pleasure of seeing another of her sons crowned. As might be expected, there was resistance to John, and much of this came from the lords of Normandy, especially as they were encouraged by King Philip of France who wished to reclaim full authority over his lands. It had long been a desire of the French kings to take Normandy away from the English throne. The Fourth Crusade was in progress and some of the knights there could have been expected to support John, judging from the support he received from them when Richard was in captivity. On the other hand, it is unknown what success Philip would have had with those same knights. John was not successful in keeping control of all the lands he claimed as King. Perhaps contributing to his divided attention was the fact that he was newly married.

John had married Isabel (also known as Hawise, Eleanor and Joan) in 1189, but he had divorced her in 1199, partly because they had no children. The divorce was allowed by the Catholic Church because of consanguinity, as they were both great-grand children of English King Henry I. A few months later John met and married Isabella, a 12 year old. This was the spark that started the rebellion against John by the French nobility who attacked Poitou where John's mother Eleanor lived. John ordered his English vassals to join him in defending the Queen Mother, but on such short notice and with probable great expense, they refused. John went to her aid anyway with a small army and brilliantly rescued her, and at the same time captured his only serious competition for the kinship, his nephew Arthur of Brittany. He placed Arthur in a prison where he later died days before his 16th birthday. There are some writers who fault John (often known as "softsword") for his losses on the continent, but it must be noted that "although a perfectly able strategist, he would always make the percentage play, opening himself to the charge of cowardice". Except for the expedition to rescue his mother, John never really took a chance like his brothers did. He calculated his strengths and weaknesses and took the "safe" route in every other endeavor of his life. We can see this pattern in his military decisions. John was repeatedly summoned to the court of Philip to give homage for his French lands, and John repeatedly ignored these believing that some of his holdings were his through direct inheritance of lands not under the authority of the French crown.

Philip attacked Normandy and in short order succeeded in conquering several key strong points. So in 1200 John signed the Treaty of Le Goulet by which he lost control of Normandy, Anjou, Maine, Poitou and Touraine. On the continent, he kept only the Channel Islands and Aquitaine, the homeland of his mother. He journeyed there to be with Eleanor, to strengthen his ties to Aquitaine--and perhaps to investigate avenues of intrigue to regain the lost lands. It is reported that in 1203, the imprisoned Arthur of Brittany died at the hands of John himself, and his weighted body sunk beneath the waves. At the time it was known that Arthur had died, but it was only after John's death that one person claimed to have witnessed the murder. John returned to England and settled affairs there, facing weaker opposition to his rule. In 1204 Eleanor died at the age of 80.

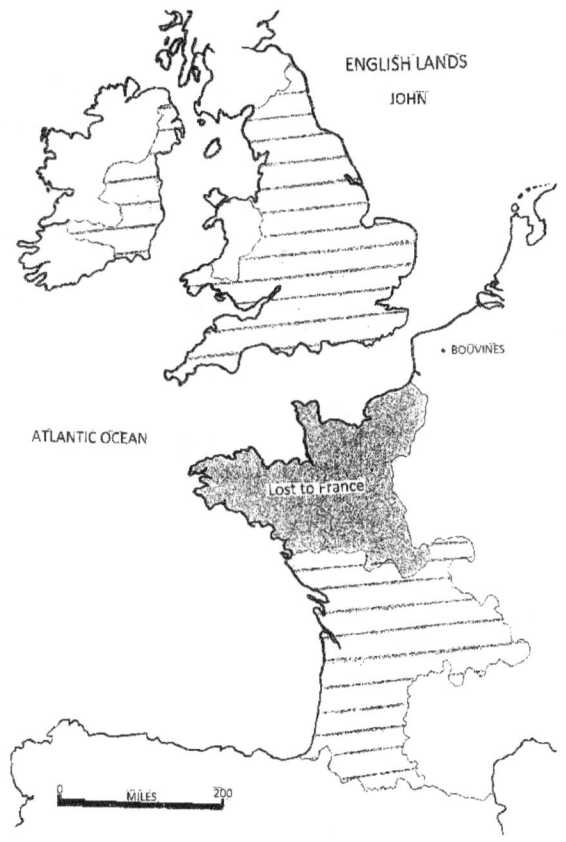

With the signing of the treaty of Le Goulet, John no longer had any feudal obligations to the King of France, and that could be viewed as a good thing. For the barons of England it created a dilemma. They too held lands on the continent, and they would lose them unless they pledged fealty to the French King for those lands. Each lord had to calculate the value and importance of his land holdings to decide to which monarch he would remain loyal. William Marshal decided to try to remain loyal to both sovereigns, by pledging allegiance to both kings. His sense of honesty and the fact that he was an important person for both Kings meant that he had to seek permission from each to do this. Surprisingly, John allowed William to pledge to Philip for his holdings in France, while remaining subject to John for his holdings in England. Philip also allowed the arrangement. Before long, John would greatly regret this permission.

John was English in his sympathies, and he devoted himself to administering it. During 1204-1205 John began raising money and support for a military expedition to conquer Normandy. Gaining Normandy by this method would free John from the obligation of kneeling before the French King in homage. However, William Marshal and many of the English lords refused to support John in this expedition. They were fully prepared to defend England from French attack, but they refused to attack France because they owed allegiance to King Philip for their lands in Normandy. John was very upset about this, but he did thoroughly understand the feudal code relating to these oaths.

Even so, John broke off his relationships with Marshal who returned to his lands in Wales and Ireland.

John had never settled down in any particular place. He was a nomad by choice and by experience. He had now been king for a few years, and he continued his nomadic ways. He traveled throughout his English realm, and that made his movements a popular spectacle. The common people now had the honor of seeing the King for themselves. His cavalcade included all the trappings and equipment of a reigning monarch.

There were tents, eating utensils, national records, an extensive library (John read books constantly), religious equipment (John never attended services himself), and all the people and animals necessary to make a government work. John often traveled to a different place without warning, making his staff scramble to provide what he needed when he needed it. He depended on the "hospitality" of the barons and lords in the locations where he happened to be. He inspected records, observed procedures and gave orders to whomever he thought needed corrections or instructions leaving little to the administrative initiative of his now micro-managed barons. John especially loved acting as supreme judge for legal disputes. He expressed an avid interest in justice and civil litigation issues he encountered in his travels. He was called "beauclerc" because of his scholarship. John once pardoned a child who had thrown a rock that killed a playmate. But there was a darker side to John's travels. It is said that no woman was safe with him. He is accused of violating the wife or daughter or sister of nearly all his barons. Many other kings had seduced important women, but John's advances were universally unwanted. Matilda Briouse and her son were thrown into a prison where they starved to death for no crime but incurring the displeasure of King John. "John was a brilliant man who was undone by his own partiality for evil" one writer observed. He could not "miss the opportunity to kick a man when he was down" said another. It seemed that a major reason for his "visitations" was to force his "hosts" to make payments to his treasury. The barons were expected to give "gifts", pay bribes, fines or taxes at each whim of the King. Most of the barons owed very large sums to him, which he did not immediately collect, so they were in terror of their own financial ruin. John could, and would, suddenly require the payment of those fees at any time.

In 1207 John began earnestly raising funds for the re-taking of Normandy. This was the same year that

Stephen Langton was called by Pope Innocent III to leave Paris and move to Rome. John's son Henry was also born in 1207. To raise funds, John placed a 1/13 tax on virtually everything, he sold writs in the nation's courts, and fines increased. He confiscated the property of those found to be guilty of various crimes, especially crimes associated with the forests. By John's reign, one-third of the land in England was in a declared forest. Nobody could enter the forests without permission, even to collect dead wood for heat or cooking. John made the penalties regarding the forest law especially harsh. People were imprisoned, blinded, even killed for the crime of "deforestation". Of course, many of these penalties could be forgiven if a sufficient bribe was paid. The forest law was a major source of income for John's coffers. Europe was experiencing inflationary times due to discovery of new silver mines, and that put pressure on John to raise even more money because prices were rising. "Customary payments" such as when an eldest son was knighted or when a daughter was married increased sometimes tenfold. The king would essentially auction off a widow or heiress to the highest bidder, or he would take a bribe not to force a marriage against her will. Minors with inheritances had their lands used by the king, or used by others who paid for that privilege. Rather than being the protector of his subject's property, he was using all the creative talents he possessed to take those properties. Especially between 1208 and 1211, John was extremely cruel, impoverishing great families and extorting huge amounts from Jews who he insisted were under his protection.

In the summer of 1205 Archbishop of Canterbury Hubert Walter died. Walter had been a friend of King Richard, and he had traveled with Richard on the crusade. When Walter died, John at first did nothing to replace him. The practice had been that the king would nominate a person, the cloister at Canterbury would elect an Archbishop, and the Pope would invest him with the symbols of his authority. Instead of nominating a man to take Walter's place, John began administering the lands under the archbishopric as his own, taking the wealth for his own treasury. In 1207 John appointed Walter de Gray to become the new archbishop, and almost immediately some in the cloister at Canterbury nominated their prior Reginald for the same office. Delegates representing both men were sent to Pope Innocent, who rejected both nominees on technicalities and appointed Stephen Langton who had only recently been summoned to Rome, and who had just become a Cardinal. Langton was then sent to England to take possession of the office, but John refused to allow him to serve. In 1208 there was a lunar eclipse in England, and many in the country expected some great calamity to follow. It came in the form of an interdict. Pope Innocent III tried to use the interdict to motivate John to recognize Stephen Langton as the new Archbishop.

Interdict is a significant weapon in the hands of a pope. Interdict means that the churches were closed to the people of a country. Only the anointing of the dying, confession and baptism of babies was permitted. Marriages and funerals would not be officiated by a priest. Marriages could be held, but not inside the church. People were buried outside of consecrated cemeteries.

It is said that John laughed at the interdict. He expelled the monks of Canterbury as Langton went into exile in France. John confiscated the property held by monasteries and churches--property like barns, fishponds and fields. This impoverished these institutions while it enriched John. John appointed his agents to manage the church properties and the clerics received only a small allowance. If the churchmen paid a high ransom, they could get their lands back, but there was no guarantee that the lands would not be taken again by the king later. According to the wishes of the Pope, clergymen were not to be married, but in England this had not been the practice for hundreds of years. John arrested the wives, mistresses and children of clerics and held them in prisons until a ransom was paid. Church law said it was evil to charge interest on loans (usury), so very few Christians were in the business of banking. Jews traditionally performed that function. John exacted very heavy fees from the Jews in exchange for his "protection". One banker was arrested by order of the king, and a "check tooth" was knocked out each day until he paid a sum of 10,000 silver marks. He finally submitted on the seventh day. So much wealth of England was in the hands of the king that there was a shortage of coins in the country.

    The fate of Matilda Briouze and her son has already been mentioned. Her husband William was from a family that had been close associates of the English kings since William the Conqueror. William Briouze was a close supporter of John. But John began to irrationally think that William was potentially a threat. Over a ten year period, the Briouze family had amassed a large (paper) debt of over 3,000 pounds of silver. Suddenly John demanded full payment, and William was unable to pay so John removed all his government offices and privileges while his property was raided by mercenaries sent by King John. That is when his wife and son were placed in prison. William was able to escape to Ireland where he found refuge with William Marshal. John began to shift his attention away from Normandy and focus his sights on Ireland in 1210.

The war in Ireland was aimed at rebellious Irish chieftains and on barons whom John felt were his enemies. Because he harbored William Briouze, William Marshal was in danger of being one of those enemies of the king. Marshal went to England to try to patch up his broken relationship with John. He had to surrender several estates in England and Ireland to the king and give hostages which included his own son. Reconciliation was made, and William Marshal was once again traveling with John while at war in Ireland.

After this, Wales was the next target of John's wrath. Marshal again surrendered estates to the king, and the traditionally war-like Welsh were temporarily defeated. Soon however, the Welsh began hit and run raids on John's estates. Furthermore, a letter was discovered that indicated that a general Welch uprising was being planned. In response, the paranoid and insecure King John demanded hostages from all his own barons, and he hired a significant number of new mercenaries to prepare for the impending war. It was now 1212, and the interdict was apparently not effective. Pope Innocent now imposed excommunication on John. This meant that he was forbidden to participate in any religious service--a penalty that had absolutely no effect on the king, but it also meant that he was now seen by the Pope as an illegitimate monarch. His own barons were under no obligation to obey him, and foreign powers could attack him with blessings from the Pope. The English barons began to avoid contact with John when it was possible. The barons were in bondage to him, but the threat of invasion from France was real and significant. In May of 1213, the English fleet under John's half brother William de Longespee destroyed a

French fleet in the Flemish harbor of Damme that was preparing for an invasion of England. Immediately before this, John took the extraordinary step of submitting to Pope Innocent through a Papal representative, and became the pope's vassal. England was now the property of the Pope. John had calculated the risks and benefits, and he had accordingly placed himself under the protection of the Church in order to avoid invasion and war with France. Innocent lifted the interdict, and the new Archbishop of Canterbury Stephen Langton arrived to take his office, present John with a beautiful gem-encrusted ring, and bring news that excommunication was also removed.

Chapter 9

CONFRONTATION AT RUNNYMEDE

Pope Innocent's controversy with King John was concerning the appointment of an archbishop at Canterbury. An interdict had lasted in England for seven years and seemed to have no effect. When an interdict had earlier been imposed on France, King Philip submitted in just over one year. The excommunication of such a pagan as John seemed to the Pope to be of minor potential effectiveness as well. Innocent was looking for a way to end this long conflict in a way that would most likely be resolved to the advantage of the Church. The Church needed the income it had lost by John's actions, the devout people of England needed the continued services of the clergy and Innocent needed the prestige of winning another battle of Church over State. When John became the Pope's vassal, all those goals seemed to be accomplished, and a key player in the Pope's plan would be Archbishop of Canterbury, Stephen Langton.

Before John's submission, the pope declared England to be "the lawful spoil of whoever could wrest them from his (John's) unhallowed hands". King Philip decided to be that "whoever" and he raised an army and 1,700 ships. Philip also had the blessing of several English bishops including Stephen Langton who was then in exile. Such an undertaking could not be called off quickly, nor was Philip desirous to do so. In response John raised an army of 60,000 and ordered every ship capable of carrying six horses or more to assemble at Portsmouth. The English people and barons responded to this appeal out of patriotism, not love for the king. But the odds were in France's favor, especially when John considered the level of loyalty that he could expect from his barons. That is when he decided to submit to the Pope. He acknowledged Innocent as his lord, acknowledged Langton as Archbishop, other bishops were recalled, and he expected the interdict and excommunications to be lifted. The impending war with France would be called off.

Langton came back to England, and John met his caravan July 20, 1213, threw himself on the ground before Archbishop Stephen and with broken voice begged for mercy and forgiveness. Langton and the other bishops were moved to tears. They all proceeded to London where John publicly promised to protect the church, renew all the good old laws (specifically mentioning King Edward the Confessor), annul evil laws and "before next Easter make restitution of confiscated property". Langton absolved John's sins, and the Eucharist was celebrated for the first time in six years. John promised to go on a crusade. This promise was to take advantage of ecclesiastical (church) law that protected any crusader from arrest or retribution of any kind, because John had ample reason to think his barons intended evil against him. He was right.

In August Langton met with some of the barons in a closed meeting where he showed them the Coronation Charter from 1100. (See the appendix for a copy of this charter). At that meeting the focus of the barons changed from intent to assassinate or overthrow the king to forcing him to sign a document similar to the charter that Henry I had been forced to sign. "With very great joy the barons swore that they would fight for these liberties, to the death if necessary, and the Archbishop promised to help with all his might." The plight of England was much like the oppression suffered under William Rufus. The solution then had been to kill the king, but with Stephen Langton's guidance and the example of Henry I Charter, the barons saw the advantages of placing the rule of law over the king. Civil wars like the Anarchy were destructive to a nation. Evil kings would rise again and again, and unless the office of king was restricted there would be no lasting solution to the problem of abuse of power by monarchs.

At Christmas 1213 the barons confronted the king and offered a charter, most likely written by Archbishop Stephen. John needed time to concentrate his defenses and organize his forces against this threat to his kingship. He pleaded for more time to consider this "complex issue" asking to wait until Easter 1214. The barons relented but demanded surety in the form of hostages so John offered Archbishop Stephen, the Bishop of Ely, and William Marshal--all close advisors and men he considered to have some degree of loyalty to him. This was agreeable to the barons. Over the next few months, John tried to find allies for his cause by contacting the barons who had not made the demands, the Pope, and certain powers on the continent where he arranged for more mercenary soldiers. His efforts were seriously short on attracting (or bullying for) the level of support he needed. The city of London closed its gates to the king, and the rebellious barons used the city as their military base to resist the king. At the meeting on Easter, "a certain schedule" was presented to King John by the barons led by Robert FitzWalter. These demands were written by Langton as they were based on the 1100 AD document he had read to the baron's months earlier. These demands were the basis of the Magna Carta. Langton and William Marshal tried to persuade John to accept the demands, but John refused. Instead, John proposed that the issues be arbitrated by a council of eight barons and presided over by the Pope. The barons rejected this proposal so on May 5, 1214 the group of barons renounced their homage and fealty to King John, convinced that a basic overhaul of the government was needed. By that time it was evident to them that John had manipulated the Pope and the chivalric code for his own protection and advantage.

The rebel barons maintained communication with the king, as they desired a reform of government and restraint on the powers of the king. This point cannot be overstated. This was the first time in England where rebels were standing for a principle rather than fighting for the interests of a person. None of the leading rebels expressed a desire to become the next ruler of the nation. They wished to establish rules of good government. "John had used his powers in an arbitrary...and exploitive fashion...(using) law to deliberately weaken and menace his lords". Over the next months there were evidently serious negotiations taking place between the barons on one side and the king--probably represented by Archbishop Langton--on the other. While this was happening, battles were fought between the two sides, but no decisive military advantage was gained. England was in a civil war.

June 15, 1215 King John and his advisors (including Langton and Marshal) met with the barons on the fields known as Runnymede. Due pomp and dignity were evident as the various barons and the despised king met for resolution of the conflict. John placed his seal on the "Charter of Rights" document we now call Magna Carta. (See the appendix for the text of the Charter). John could have signed the document, but many among the barons were not literate and the tradition was for seals of the signer to be used instead. Colored wax and colorful ribbons accompanied the actual seal, and these were much more impressive than a simple signature. With John's seal, a "quasi pax" (sort of peace) was restored in England, and now a *written* contract between the king and his barons existed. However, John had no intention of honoring the charter any more than he had been influenced by his excommunication by the Pope. Pope Innocent III, in fact, condemned the Magna Carta because it infringed upon the power of his sworn vassal, King John. Innocent's proclamation said

> "On behalf of Almighty God, Father, Son and Holy Spirit, and by the authority of Ss. Peter and Paul His apostles, and by our own authority, acting on the general advice of our brethren, we utterly reject and condemn this settlement and under threat of excommunication we order that the king should not dare to observe it and that the barons and their associates should not require it to be observed: The charter, with all undertakings and guarantees whether confirming it or resulting from it, we declare it to be null and void of all validity forever. Wherefore, let no man deem it lawful to infringe this document of our annulment and prohibition or presume to oppose it. If anyone presume to do so, let him know that he will incur the anger of Almighty God and of Ss. Peter and Paul His apostles."

This proclamation was not well known in England. Stephen Langton was in charge of producing copies for the barons and people, but he did not do so. He had not been part of the "general advice of our brethren" mentioned in the Papal pronouncement, and Langton intended to speak with the Pope personally when he went to Rome soon after the Charter was agreed upon. Innocent had summoned all the Bishops for a great council (the 4th Lateran Council) to address several important theological and procedural issues facing the Church. By the time he was leaving to attend the council, Papal Legate Pandolf had in the name of the Pope, suspended Langton from the Archbishopric for his refusal to proclaim the Pope's condemnation. True to the principles he had first voiced while in Paris, Langton ignored the suspension and set off for Rome. He intended to argue that the Pope had issued the condemnation based on wrong information about the charter, and that Pandolf was not the lawful representative of the Pope in England. In 1125 Pope Honorius II had proclaimed the Archbishop of Canterbury was his representative. Langton was also opposed to the appointment of foreigners to church offices in England who very often did not even visit their canonries, yet they collected funds from them by using hired clergy. In essence, this arrangement was a form of papal tax collection that drained significant funds from the people of England. These were also issues Langton wished to take up with the Pope at the Lateran Council.

In 1214 John had created a coalition of powers to accomplish what he certainly could not accomplish on his own. Otto, German Emperor of the Holy Roman Empire was John's nephew, and greedy for more territory at the expense of France. The Count of Flanders wanted full separation of Flanders from feudal obligations to the French King, and a bit of French soil would make the situation even better. These two leaders and a few other lords who were discontent with

Philip were set to attack France from the north while John and an army of Englishmen and mercenaries attacked from the south. King Philip was forced to divide his army to meet these two simultaneous threats, so he personally took an army to meet the northern threat while his young son Louis (age 27) led an army to stop or at least slow the threat from John who had landed in the south. The battle at Bouvines (July 25, 1214) was decisive. Fought around a bridge on muddy ground, the greater numbers commanded by Emperor Otto were not well coordinated with the Flemish. The battle lasted four or five hours, and Philip was unhorsed by a pike man wielding a hooked pike that pulled him from his mount. Philip would have been killed had it not been for the actions of his loyal bodyguard. The Count of Flanders was captured, and Otto was fortunate to escape. Seven hundred mercenaries from Brabant were captured by the French and executed. Louis was able to keep John's army from aiding his allies. The grand plan was ruined, so John and his army were forced to return to England humiliated and impoverished, "all his taxation gone to waste". Had John won this campaign, there would have not been a Magna Carta, France would have been weakened, Flanders and the German Empire strengthened. Instead, John returned to England very much weakened, his barons emboldened. Because of the loss on the field of Bouvines, John was forced to yield on the field of Runnymede.

Chapter 10

AFTER RUNNYMEDE

When the Magna Carta was sealed, that was not the end of the story. England was still in a civil war because the barons and John were still at odds. This war was not hot and furious, the Charter had provided a framework for peace, but one could not say there was peace in the realm. Also, the French were on the march, and they were in the process of invading England. William Marshal was at John's side, prepared to stand in defense of the king and the realm against the French.
 The barons were organizing themselves to conform to the provision in the Charter that twenty-five of their number be chosen to see to it that John obey its provisions. The barons were also preparing to defend against France, though some did this with a certain lack of enthusiasm because of their fealty oaths to the French king. Stephen Langton was going to Rome to attend the Fourth Lateran Council as a Cardinal, even though he knew that Pope Innocent III had removed his appointment as Archbishop of Canterbury. He was hopeful that he could speak with Innocent about the Magna Carta and other matters concerning the English Church. He would not return to his Archbishopric until 1218.
   Leading an army of mercenaries and Englishmen, John fought against the French. Marshal was his trusted chief military officer. When London was threatened by the French, (under Prince Louis), Marshal courageously counterattacked winning the situation. Since Innocent still considered England to be his

domain, he pressured France to withdraw. This alone made it more difficult for France to recruit allies, and easier for John to recruit mercenaries. For once, John was on the "right" side. Slowly the French were forced out of England. There were times John was threatened by his opponents, but there seemed to be success on the horizon. John was ill, probably with dysentery, and he was traveling to another location with his entire retinue. Night was near, and there was a shortcut to their destination available, across a "low tide only" path.

Perhaps because of his illness he was not thinking straight. Perhaps the order to move came a bit late, or the baggage train was late for some reason. At any rate the baggage train was caught when the tide came in. The ground beneath them began turning soft, then it transformed into quicksand. With the tide completely in, there was no remnant of it at all. All of John's precious things were completely lost, including a sizeable portion of his treasury. People then and since have searched for that treasure, but none have discovered it. Today it is no doubt covered by sand and water and nearly lost from the memory of man. John and some of his people escaped to Newark, but his health deteriorated further. Within days he was dead, and not quite fifty years old.

John decreed before his death that William Marshal, age 70, would be the regent for his nine year old son Henry. Marshal was not excited about the task. The chief loyalist barons pleaded that he accept, as did Gualo the Pope's emissary. In fact, Gualo offered an indulgence for all of William's sins, if he accepted the task. In 1190 Pope Innocent had officially instituted indulgences, which promised that the merits of the saints could be applied to the recipient of the indulgence. For a man of war and whose loyalties had sometimes been questioned, the indulgence probably

was an important factor in his decision to accept the appointment. The regency would be a coveted job under other circumstances. But England was still at war with a foreign power, in a civil war, the previous king was despised, and the finances of the realm were a horrible mess. Taxes had not been collected for quite a while, and John's greed and methods were hated.
Mercenaries were demanding their pay with the threat they could turn on the government if they were not paid. The regency was not a happy post under these circumstances. William Marshal at last agreed to take the regency.

Some of the mercenaries were paid and sent home. A peace treaty between France and England was negotiated after the French were defeated at Lincoln, and their navy defeated at Sandwich. Regent William then reissued the Magna Carta in 1216 as a sign that the young new king would follow the Charter. It was sealed by William as Regent and three other earls, by eighteen barons, by all seven English, and by all four Welch bishops. William was probably illiterate, as we have no evidence that he ever received an education.
But lack of education is no reason to discount intelligence, as future events would show. The wording of the 1216 Magna Carta was different from the original. There were several important omissions and a few minor changes.

The council of 25 barons was not needed, it was argued, because the new king (through his regent) was voluntarily issuing the charter. Other omissions involved various taxes and fees that the new signatories said were "so weighty that they should be decided only after long consideration by a full council of the realm". The main motivation for most of the changes was that the government needed money. Then and for many centuries in the future, the treasury of the government was the treasury of the king--and visa versa. Some of the changes were seen as necessary in the face of war. "The charter of 1216 carefully omitted the most important points of dispute between John and his barons, but it guaranteed that abuses would not be revived". William could not use the various normal fund acquisition methods for obvious reasons. With commendable wisdom, he turned to other sources of funding. There were jewels and fine clothing kept in storage in various castles. Many of these were used to pay immediate needs. One cache included a collection of rings: 18 with fine emeralds, 73 with good emeralds, 107 with sapphires, 15 with diamonds, 28 with rubies, and 9 with garnets. A portion of these was given to pay a garrison at Dover. Various silk and other expensive garments were similarly turned into needed cash. The peace with France saved money as the mercenaries hired to fight them could be paid off and sent home.

The 1216 version of Magna Carta was admittedly provisional. In 1217 a new and final version of the charter was issued. (See the appendix for the text of this version of Magna Carta). This version of the Charter was actually issued as two documents: the Charter of Liberties, and the Forest Charter. The Charter of Liberties was nearly exactly like the 1216 Magna Carta, with only minor changes and additions, with the exception of the thirty-ninth article, and the last six were new. The common principle in these was a strengthening of the position of the king and the nobles, though the newest castles were to be destroyed. The Forest Charter ordered the deforestation of lands made forests by Richard and John. Barons and clergy passing through the remaining forests were allowed to kill two wild animals if they sounded a horn. Pardons were given to all who were imprisoned under Henry II, Richard and John as long as they could provide surety for good behavior in the future. Nobody would lose life or limb for breaking the forest laws in the future. This 1217 version of the Charter declared that it would be binding on all future kings, just like the earlier ones had, but it technically needed the Great Seal of the realm to actually make it binding. Evidently, Regent William and the other barons involved were content to wait until young Henry III reached the age of majority for that to happen. In the meantime, the Regent appointed John Marshal as the person to enforce the new forest laws. This John Marshal's father, son of William, had been a signatory on the first Magna Carta.

William's main focus became re-establishing a strong financial basis for the nation. He also had to rebuild the judicial system that had collapsed when John died. Because of his integrity and the respect he held, Regent Marshal was able to see a degree of success in these two areas. "William's great quality was that most intangible one--character". The aging warrior was showing himself capable of wisely governing, but he was also wearing out physically. Late in 1218 he said "I can do no more for God than to give myself to Him, repenting all my sins" demonstrating an awareness of his final days on earth. His final illness was weeks in length, and he called for his wife and children to his bedside on more than one occasion. Finally in 1219, the great knight died.

At William Marshal's funeral important barons from all around attended as Archbishop Stephen Langton officiated. Part of the final remarks Stephen pronounced included these comments directed to those who remained:

"Lords, you see what the life of the world is worth. When one is dead, one is no longer more than a bit of earth. Behold all that remains of the best knight who ever lived. You will all come to this. Each man dies on his day. We have here our mirror, you and I. Let each man say his paternoster that God may receive this Christian into His glory and place him among His faithful vassals, as he so well deserves."

And so it was. And so it still is today. We are born, we live our lives, then "after this the judgment" of God.

Langton had returned in 1218 from Rome having been away for about three years. He had attended the 4th Lateran Council, but probably never got an audience with Innocent, who was ill. Pope Innocent died in 1216 and was replaced by Pope Honorius III who reinstated Langton as Archbishop of Canterbury. Stephen's brother Simon was made Archdeacon of Canterbury, and he lived for another twenty years becoming a widely respected theologian in his own right. Stephen continued to argue for his rights as official representative of the Pope in England. His relationship with Honorius was excellent, but no official changes were made until Pandulf resigned in 1221. In 1222 Archbishop Stephen convened a council in Osney to introduce and apply the decrees and changes in ecclesiastical laws that had been decided at the 4th Lateran Council. This began a new era in English church law. He turned his attention to being a close advisor to King Henry III. Langton was made chairman of a council of barons that had the power to raise funds for the defense of the kingdom. In 1223 Langton sickened and died. He was buried at Canterbury. In 1225 Henry III reissued the 1217 version of the Magna

Carta as a symbol of the unity of government and assurance that Henry would rule wisely. By 1227 Henry was independent of his advisors and realistically independent from vassalage to the Pope.

At intervals of years the Magna Carta was reissued. Sometimes it was ordered to be read in the churches of the realm. One hundred and fifty years after it was issued, it was translated into English. The principle of written law, the legal equivalent of the Bible, became imbedded in the minds of Englishmen. Eventually, those principles were applied to the legal system of the American colonies and to the United States Constitution. Today, it may even be said that the Magna Carta is more highly regarded in the United States than in the United Kingdom. It came about because of the depravity of a King, the pious wisdom of a clergyman and the wise regency of a respected knight 800 years ago, June 15, 1215.

POSTSCRIPT

And they all died, though the document that they wrote continued on for now 800 years. We must also die, and that is the great problem of humanity. No one desires to live like John with a horrible reputation and for whom our sense of justice demands that he get his due punishment after death. Evil must be punished. We might identify with Marshal who faithfully and wisely did his duty, loyal to his superiors and his own sense of right. But Marshal himself faced death with dread and fear of judgment for the men he killed and people he wronged while performing his duties. He was unsure of his eternal destiny as he took his last breath. Langton also had to face the end of his life with a realization that he must face the exacting, perfect standards of God. His knowledge of scripture actually placed him in a more accountable spot, because he knew himself well and the holiness of heaven better than others.

So what DOES the Bible say about the evil we have done and how we can face the Holy Judge of the universe? First we must agree with God that we are not perfect. We may know someone who thinks he is perfect, but we can see that he is not. We simply need to apply that knowledge to ourselves. "All have sinned and come short of the glory of God" (Romans 3:23).

"There is none righteous, no, not one" (Romans 3:10). Next, we must see our sins as God does. "The wages of sin is death" (Romans 6:23). We fail to meet the standard of moral perfection (Matthew 5:48), God must punish that sin. To do less would make him an unjust judge. This impossible human dilemma was resolved when the perfect God became a human, lived a perfect life, and then paid the penalty (death) not for his own transgressions but for ours. "All we, like sheep, have gone astray, we have turned every one to his own way, but the Lord has laid on Him (Jesus) the sin of us all" (Isaiah 53:6). So the "wages of sin" was paid, and the payment is put on our account if we simply agree to the arrangement. This is the supreme gift. "For by grace we are saved through faith, and that not of ourselves, it is the gift of God, not of works lest any man should boast" (Ephesians 2:8-9). We can be forgiven.

Believe that Jesus paid the penalty for your sins, ask in faith through prayer that Jesus' payment be put on your account, and seek His help in turning away (repenting) from the continued practice of sin. In a sentence this is the great transaction that will solve the problem of sin as we face death. There is more to Christianity than this; one can spend a lifetime learning and applying the truths of the Bible in one's life. But you can believe immediately, you can silently pray to God even right now and start the journey of peace with God, forgiven. I hope and pray that you do.

APPENDIX

Coronation Charter 1100

Henry, king of the English, to Bishop Samson and Urso de Abetot and all his barons and faithful, both French and English, of Worcestershire, greeting.
1. Know that by the mercy of God and the common counsel of the barons of the whole kingdom of England I have been crowned king of said kingdom; and because the kingdom had been oppressed by unjust exactions, I, through fear of God and the love which I have toward you all, in the first place make the holy church of God free, so that I will neither sell nor put to farm, nor on the death of archbishop or bishop or abbot will I take anything from the church's demesne or from its men until the successor shall enter it. And I take away all the bad customs by which the kingdom of England was unjustly oppressed; which bad customs I here set down in part:
2. If any of my barons, earls, or others who hold of me shall have died, his heir shall not buy back his land as he used to do in the time of my brother, but he shall relieve it by a just and lawful relief. Likewise also the men of my barons shall relieve their lands from their lords by a just and lawful relief.
3. And if any of my barons or other men should wish to give his daughter, sister, niece, or kinswoman in marriage, let him speak with me about it; but I will neither take anything from him for this permission nor prevent his giving her unless he should be minded to

join her to my enemy. And if, upon the death of a baron or other of my men, a daughter is left as heir, I will give her with her land by the advice of my barons. And if, on the death of her husband, the wife is left and without children, she shall have her dowry and right of marriage, and I will not give her to a husband unless according to her will.

4. But if a wife be left with children, she shall indeed have her dowry and right of marriage so long as she shall keep her body lawfully, and I will not give her unless according to her will. And the guardian of the land and children shall be either the wife or another of the relatives who more justly ought to be. And I command that my barons restrain themselves similarly in dealing with the sons and daughters or wives of their men.

5. The common seigniorage, which has been taken through the cities and counties, but which was not taken in the time of King Edward I absolutely forbid henceforth. If anyone, whether a moneyer or other, be taken with false money, let due justice be done for it.

6. I remit all pleas and all debts which were owing to my brother, except my lawful fixed revenues and except those amounts which had been agreed upon for the inheritances of others or for things which more justly concerned others. And if anyone had pledged anything for his own inheritance, I remit it; also all reliefs which had been agreed upon for just inheritances.

7. And if any of my barons or men shall grow feeble, as he shall give or arrange to give his money, I grant that it be so given. But if, prevented by arms or sickness, he shall not have given or arranged to give his money, his wife, children, relatives, or lawful men shall distribute it for the good of his soul as shall seem best to them.

8. If any of my barons or men commit a crime, he shall not bind himself to a payment at the king's mercy as he has been doing in the time of my father or my brother; but he shall make amends according to the extent of the crime as he would have done before the time of my father in the time of my other predecessors. But if he be convicted of treachery or heinous crime, he shall make amends as is just.

9. I forgive all murders committed before the day I was crowned king; and those which shall be committed in the future shall be justly compensated according to the law of King Edward.

10. By the common consent of my barons I have kept in my hands forests as my father had them.

11. To those knights who render military service for their lands I grant of my own gift that the lands of their demesne ploughs be free from all payments and all labor, so that, having been released from so great a burden, they may equip themselves well with horses and arms and be fully prepared for my service and the defense of my kingdom.

12. I impose a strict peace upon my whole kingdom and command that it be maintained henceforth.

13. I restore to you the law of King Edward with those amendments introduced into it by my father with the advice of his barons.

14. If anyone, since the death of King William my brother, has taken anything belonging to me or to anyone else, the whole is to be quickly restored without fine; but if any one keep anything of it, he upon whom it shall be found shall pay me a heavy fine.

Witnesses Maurice bishop of London, and William bishop elect of Winchester, and Gerard bishop of Hereford, and Earl Henry, and earl Simon, and Walter Giffard,and Robert de Montfort, and Roger Bigot, and Eudo the steward, and Robert son of Hamo, and Robert Malet. At London when I was crowned. Farewell.

Text of the 1215 Magna Carta

JOHN, by the grace of God King of England, Lord of Ireland, Duke of Normandy and Aquitaine, and Count of Anjou, to his archbishops, bishops, abbots, earls, barons, justices, foresters, sheriffs, stewards, servants, and to all his officials and loyal subjects, Greeting. KNOW THAT BEFORE GOD, for the health of our soul and those of our ancestors and heirs, to the honor of God, the exaltation of the holy Church, and the better ordering of our kingdom, at the advice of our reverend fathers Stephen, archbishop of Canterbury, primate of all England, and cardinal of the holy Roman Church, Henry archbishop of Dublin, William bishop of London, Peter bishop of Winchester, Jocelin bishop of Bath and Glastonbury, Hugh bishop of Lincoln, Walter Bishop of Worcester, William bishop of Coventry, Benedict bishop of Rochester, Master Pandulf subdeacon and member of the papal household, Brother Aymeric master of the knighthood of the Temple in England, William Marshal earl of Pembroke, William earl of Salisbury, William earl of Warren, William earl of Arundel, Alan de Galloway constable of Scotland, Warin Fitz Gerald, Peter Fitz Herbert, Hubert de Burgh seneschal of Poitou, Hugh de Neville, Matthew Fitz Herbert, Thomas Basset, Alan Basset, Philip Daubeny, Robert de Roppeley, John Marshal, John Fitz Hugh, and other loyal subjects:

(1) FIRST, THAT WE HAVE GRANTED TO GOD, and by this present charter have confirmed for us and our heirs in perpetuity, that the English Church shall be free, and shall have its rights undiminished, and its liberties unimpaired. That we wish this so to be observed, appears from the fact that of our own free will, before the outbreak of the present dispute between us and our barons, we granted and confirmed by charter the freedom of the Church's elections - a right reckoned to be of the greatest necessity and importance to it - and caused this to be confirmed by Pope Innocent III. This freedom we shall observe ourselves, and desire to be observed in good faith by our heirs in perpetuity.
TO ALL FREE MEN OF OUR KINGDOM we have also granted, for us and our heirs forever, all the liberties written out below, to have and to keep for them and their heirs, of us and our heirs:
(2) If any earl, baron, or other person that holds lands directly of the Crown, for military service, shall die, and at his death his heir shall be of full age and owe a 'relief', the heir shall have his inheritance on payment of the ancient scale of 'relief'. That is to say, the heir or heirs of an earl shall pay £100 for the entire earl's barony, the heir or heirs of a knight 100s. at most for the entire knight's 'fee', and any man that owes less shall pay less, in accordance with the ancient usage of 'fees'
(3) But if the heir of such a person is under age and a ward, when he comes of age he shall have his inheritance without 'relief' or fine.
(4) The guardian of the land of an heir who is under age shall take from it only reasonable revenues, customary dues, and feudal services. He shall do this without destruction or damage to men or property. If we have given the guardianship of the land to a sheriff, or to any person answerable to us for the revenues, and he

commits destruction or damage, we will exact compensation from him, and the land shall be entrusted to two worthy and prudent men of the same 'fee', who shall be answerable to us for the revenues, or to the person to whom we have assigned them. If we have given or sold to anyone the guardianship of such land, and he causes destruction or damage, he shall lose the guardianship of it, and it shall be handed over to two worthy and prudent men of the same 'fee', who shall be similarly answerable to us.

(5) For so long as a guardian has guardianship of such land, he shall maintain the houses, parks, fish preserves, ponds, mills, and everything else pertaining to it, from the revenues of the land itself. When the heir comes of age, he shall restore the whole land to him, stocked with plough teams and such implements of husbandry as the season demands and the revenues from the land can reasonably bear.

(6) Heirs may be given in marriage, but not to someone of lower social standing. Before a marriage takes place, it shall be made known to the heir's next-of-kin.

(7) At her husband's death, a widow may have her marriage portion and inheritance at once and without trouble. She shall pay nothing for her dower, marriage portion, or any inheritance that she and her husband held jointly on the day of his death. She may remain in her husband's house for forty days after his death, and within this period her dower shall be assigned to her.

(8) No widow shall be compelled to marry, so long as she wishes to remain without a husband. But she must give security that she will not marry without royal consent, if she holds her lands of the Crown, or without the consent of whatever other lord she may hold them of.

(9) Neither we nor our officials will seize any land or rent in payment of a debt, so long as the debtor has movable goods sufficient to discharge the debt. A debtor's sureties shall not be distrained upon so long as the debtor himself can discharge his debt. If, for lack of means, the debtor is unable to discharge his debt, his sureties shall be answerable for it. If they so desire, they may have the debtor's lands and rents until they have received satisfaction for the debt that they paid for him, unless the debtor can show that he has settled his obligations to them.

(10) If anyone who has borrowed a sum of money from Jews dies before the debt has been repaid, his heir shall pay no interest on the debt for so long as he remains under age, irrespective of whom he holds his lands. If such a debt falls into the hands of the Crown, it will take nothing except the principal sum specified in the bond.

(11) If a man dies owing money to Jews, his wife may have her dower and pay nothing towards the debt from it. If he leaves children that are under age, their needs may also be provided for on a scale appropriate to the size of his holding of lands. The debt is to be paid out of the residue, reserving the service due to his feudal lords. Debts owed to persons other than Jews are to be dealt with similarly.

(12) No 'scutage' or 'aid' may be levied in our kingdom without its general consent, unless it is for the ransom of our person, to make our eldest son a knight, and (once) to marry our eldest daughter. For these purposes only a reasonable 'aid' may be levied. 'Aids' from the city of London are to be treated similarly.

(13) The city of London shall enjoy all its ancient liberties and free customs, both by land and by water. We also will and grant that all other cities, boroughs,

towns, and ports shall enjoy all their liberties and free customs.

(14) To obtain the general consent of the realm for the assessment of an 'aid' - except in the three cases specified above - or a 'scutage', we will cause the archbishops, bishops, abbots, earls, and greater barons to be summoned individually by letter. To those who hold lands directly of us we will cause a general summons to be issued, through the sheriffs and other officials, to come together on a fixed day (of which at least forty days notice shall be given) and at a fixed place. In all letters of summons, the cause of the summons will be stated. When a summons has been issued, the business appointed for the day shall go forward in accordance with the resolution of those present, even if not all those who were summoned have appeared.

(15) In future we will allow no one to levy an 'aid' from his free men, except to ransom his person, to make his eldest son a knight, and (once) to marry his eldest daughter. For these purposes only a reasonable 'aid' may be levied.

(16) No man shall be forced to perform more service for a knight's 'fee', or other free holding of land, than is due from it.

(17) Ordinary lawsuits shall not follow the royal court around, but shall be held in a fixed place.

(18) Inquests of novel disseisin, mort d'ancestor, and darrein presentment shall be taken only in their proper county court. We ourselves, or in our absence abroad our chief justice, will send two justices to each county four times a year, and these justices, with four knights of the county elected by the county itself, shall hold the assizes in the county court, on the day and in the place where the court meets.

(19) If any assizes cannot be taken on the day of the county court, as many knights and freeholders shall afterwards remain behind, of those who have attended the court, as will suffice for the administration of justice, having regard to the volume of business to be done.
(20) For a trivial offence, a free man shall be fined only in proportion to the degree of his offence, and for a serious offence correspondingly, but not so heavily as to deprive him of his livelihood. In the same way, a merchant shall be spared his merchandise, and a villein the implements of his husbandry, if they fall upon the mercy of a royal court. None of these fines shall be imposed except by the assessment on oath of reputable men of the neighborhood.
(21) Earls and barons shall be fined only by their equals, and in proportion to the gravity of their offence.
(22) A fine imposed upon the lay property of a clerk in holy orders shall be assessed upon the same principles, without reference to the value of his ecclesiastical benefice.
(23) No town or person shall be forced to build bridges over rivers except those with an ancient obligation to do so.
(24) No sheriff, constable, coroners, or other royal officials are to hold lawsuits that should be held by the royal justices.
(25) Every county, hundred, wapentake, and riding shall remain at its ancient rent, without increase, except the royal demesne manors.
(26) If at the death of a man who holds a lay 'fee' of the Crown, a sheriff or royal official produces royal letters patent of summons for a debt due to the Crown, it shall be lawful for them to seize and list movable goods found in the lay 'fee' of the dead man to the value of the debt, as assessed by worthy men. Nothing shall be removed

until the whole debt is paid, when the residue shall be given over to the executors to carry out the dead man's will. If no debt is due to the Crown, all the movable goods shall be regarded as the property of the dead man, except the reasonable shares of his wife and children.

(27) If a free man dies intestate, his movable goods are to be distributed by his next-of-kin and friends, under the supervision of the Church. The rights of his debtors are to be preserved.

(28) No constable or other royal official shall take corn or other movable goods from any man without immediate payment, unless the seller voluntarily offers postponement of this.

(29) No constable may compel a knight to pay money for castle-guard if the knight is willing to undertake the guard in person, or with reasonable excuse to supply some other fit man to do it. A knight taken or sent on military service shall be excused from castle-guard for the period of this service.

(30) No sheriff, royal official, or other person shall take horses or carts for transport from any free man, without his consent.

(31) Neither we nor any royal official will take wood for our castle, or for any other purpose, without the consent of the owner.

(32) We will not keep the lands of people convicted of felony in our hand for longer than a year and a day, after which they shall be returned to the lords of the 'fees' concerned.

(33) All fish-weirs shall be removed from the Thames, the Medway, and throughout the whole of England, except on the sea coast.

(34) The writ called precipe shall not in future be issued to anyone in respect of any holding of land, if a free man

could thereby be deprived of the right of trial in his own lord's court.

(35) There shall be standard measures of wine, ale, and corn (the London quarter), throughout the kingdom. There shall also be a standard width of dyed cloth, russet, and haberject, namely two ells within the selvedges. Weights are to be standardized similarly.

(36) In future nothing shall be paid or accepted for the issue of a writ of inquisition of life or limbs. It shall be given gratis, and not refused.

(37) If a man holds land of the Crown by 'fee-farm', 'socage', or 'burgage', and also holds land of someone else for knight's service, we will not have guardianship of his heir, nor of the land that belongs to the other person's 'fee', by virtue of the 'fee-farm', 'socage', or 'burgage', unless the 'fee-farm' owes knight's service. We will not have the guardianship of a man's heir, or of land that he holds of someone else, by reason of any small property that he may hold of the Crown for a service of knives, arrows, or the like.

(38) In future no official shall place a man on trial upon his own unsupported statement, without producing credible witnesses to the truth of it.

(39) No free man shall be seized or imprisoned, or stripped of his rights or possessions, or outlawed or exiled, or deprived of his standing in any other way, nor will we proceed with force against him, or send others to do so, except by the lawful judgment of his equals or by the law of the land.

(40) To no one will we sell, to no one deny or delay right or justice.

(41) All merchants may enter or leave England unharmed and without fear, and may stay or travel within it, by land or water, for purposes of trade, free from all illegal exactions, in accordance with ancient and

lawful customs. This, however, does not apply in time of war to merchants from a country that is at war with us. Any such merchants found in our country at the outbreak of war shall be detained without injury to their persons or property, until we or our chief justice have discovered how our own merchants are being treated in the country at war with us. If our own merchants are safe they shall be safe too.

(42) In future it shall be lawful for any man to leave and return to our kingdom unharmed and without fear, by land or water, preserving his allegiance to us, except in time of war, for some short period, for the common benefit of the realm. People that have been imprisoned or outlawed in accordance with the law of the land, people from a country that is at war with us, and merchants - who shall be dealt with as stated above - are excepted from this provision.

(43) If a man holds lands of any 'escheat' such as the 'honor' of Wallingford, Nottingham, Boulogne, Lancaster, or of other 'escheats' in our hand that are baronies, at his death his heir shall give us only the 'relief' and service that he would have made to the baron, had the barony been in the baron's hand. We will hold the 'escheat' in the same manner as the baron held it.

(44) People who live outside the forest need not in future appear before the royal justices of the forest in answer to general summonses, unless they are actually involved in proceedings or are sureties for someone who has been seized for a forest offence.

(45) We will appoint as justices, constables, sheriffs, or other officials, only men that know the law of the realm and are minded to keep it well.

(46) All barons who have founded abbeys, and have charters of English kings or ancient tenure as evidence

of this, may have guardianship of them when there is no abbot, as is their due.

(47) All forests that have been created in our reign shall at once be disafforested. River-banks that have been enclosed in our reign shall be treated similarly.

(48) All evil customs relating to forests and warrens, foresters, warreners, sheriffs and their servants, or river-banks and their wardens, are at once to be investigated in every county by twelve sworn knights of the county, and within forty days of their enquiry the evil customs are to be abolished completely and irrevocably. But we, or our chief justice if we are not in England, are first to be informed.

(49) We will at once return all hostages and charters delivered up to us by Englishmen as security for peace or for loyal service.

(50) We will remove completely from their offices the kinsmen of Gerard de Athée, and in future they shall hold no offices in England. The people in question are Engelard de Cigogné, Peter, Guy, and Andrew de Chanceaux, Guy de Cigogné, Geoffrey de Martigny and his brothers, Philip Marc and his brothers, with Geoffrey his nephew, and all their followers.

(51) As soon as peace is restored, we will remove from the kingdom all the foreign knights, bowmen, their attendants, and the mercenaries that have come to it, to its harm, with horses and arms.

(52) To any man whom we have deprived or dispossessed of lands, castles, liberties, or rights, without the lawful judgment of his equals, we will at once restore these. In cases of dispute the matter shall be resolved by the judgment of the twenty-five barons referred to below in the clause for securing the peace. In cases, however, where a man was deprived or dispossessed of something without the lawful judgment

of his equals by our father King Henry or our brother King Richard, and it remains in our hands or is held by others under our warranty, we shall have respite for the period commonly allowed to Crusaders, unless a lawsuit had been begun, or an enquiry had been made at our order, before we took the Cross as a Crusader. On our return from the Crusade, or if we abandon it, we will at once render justice in full.

(53) We shall have similar respite in rendering justice in connection with forests that are to be disafforested, or to remain forests, when these were first afforested by our father Henry or our brother Richard; with the guardianship of lands in another person's 'fee', when we have hitherto had this by virtue of a 'fee' held of us for knight's service by a third party; and with abbeys founded in another person's 'fee', in which the lord of the 'fee' claims to own a right. On our return from the Crusade, or if we abandon it, we will at once do full justice to complaints about these matters.

(54) No one shall be arrested or imprisoned on the appeal of a woman for the death of any person except her husband.

(55) All fines that have been given to us unjustly and against the law of the land, and all fines that we have exacted unjustly, shall be entirely remitted or the matter decided by a majority judgment of the twenty-five barons referred to below in the clause for securing the peace together with Stephen, archbishop of Canterbury, if he can be present, and such others as he wishes to bring with him. If the archbishop cannot be present, proceedings shall continue without him, provided that if any of the twenty-five barons has been involved in a similar suit himself, his judgment shall be set aside, and someone else chosen and sworn in his place, as a

substitute for the single occasion, by the rest of the twenty-five.

(56) If we have deprived or dispossessed any Welshmen of lands, liberties, or anything else in England or in Wales, without the lawful judgment of their equals, these are at once to be returned to them. A dispute on this point shall be determined in the Marches by the judgment of equals. English law shall apply to holdings of land in England, Welsh law to those in Wales, and the law of the Marches to those in the Marches. The Welsh shall treat us and ours in the same way.

(57) In cases where a Welshman was deprived or dispossessed of anything, without the lawful judgment of his equals, by our father King Henry or our brother King Richard, and it remains in our hands or is held by others under our warranty, we shall have respite for the period commonly allowed to Crusaders, unless a lawsuit had been begun, or an enquiry had been made at our order, before we took the Cross as a Crusader. But on our return from the Crusade, or if we abandon it, we will at once do full justice according to the laws of Wales and the said regions.

(58) We will at once return the son of Llewellyn, all Welsh hostages, and the charters delivered to us as security for the peace.

(59) With regard to the return of the sisters and hostages of Alexander, king of Scotland, his liberties and his rights, we will treat him in the same way as our other barons of England, unless it appears from the charters that we hold from his father William, formerly king of Scotland, that he should be treated otherwise. This matter shall be resolved by the judgment of his equals in our court.

(60) All these customs and liberties that we have granted shall be observed in our kingdom in so far as concerns our own relations with our subjects. Let all men of our kingdom, whether clergy or laymen, observe them similarly in their relations with their own men.

(61) SINCE WE HAVE GRANTED ALL THESE THINGS for God, for the better ordering of our kingdom, and to allay the discord that has arisen between us and our barons, and since we desire that they shall be enjoyed in their entirety, with lasting strength, forever, we give and grant to the barons the following security:

The barons shall elect twenty-five of their number to keep, and cause to be observed with all their might, the peace and liberties granted and confirmed to them by this charter.

If we, our chief justice, our officials, or any of our servants offend in any respect against any man, or transgress any of the articles of the peace or of this security, and the offence is made known to four of the said twenty-five barons, they shall come to us - or in our absence from the kingdom to the chief justice - to declare it and claim immediate redress. If we, or in our absence abroad the chief justice, make no redress within forty days, reckoning from the day on which the offence was declared to us or to him, the four barons shall refer the matter to the rest of the twenty-five barons, who may distrain upon and assail us in every way possible, with the support of the whole community of the land, by seizing our castles, lands, possessions, or anything else saving only our own person and those of the queen and our children, until they have secured such redress as they have determined upon. Having secured the redress, they may then resume their normal obedience to us.

Any man who so desires may take an oath to obey the commands of the twenty-five barons for the achievement of these ends, and to join with them in assailing us to the utmost of his power. We give public and free permission to take this oath to any man who so desires, and at no time will we prohibit any man from taking it. Indeed, we will compel any of our subjects who are unwilling to take it to swear it at our command.
If one of the twenty-five barons dies or leaves the country, or is prevented in any other way from discharging his duties, the rest of them shall choose another baron in his place, at their discretion, who shall be duly sworn in as they were.
In the event of disagreement among the twenty-five barons on any matter referred to them for decision, the verdict of the majority present shall have the same validity as a unanimous verdict of the whole twenty-five, whether these were all present or some of those summoned were unwilling or unable to appear.
The twenty-five barons shall swear to obey all the above articles faithfully, and shall cause them to be obeyed by others to the best of their power.
We will not seek to procure from anyone, either by our own efforts or those of a third party, anything by which any part of these concessions or liberties might be revoked or diminished. Should such a thing be procured, it shall be null and void and we will at no time make use of it, either ourselves or through a third party.
(62) We have remitted and pardoned fully to all men any ill-will, hurt, or grudges that have arisen between us and our subjects, whether clergy or laymen, since the beginning of the dispute. We have in addition remitted fully, and for our own part have also pardoned, to all clergy and laymen any offences committed as a result of

the said dispute between Easter in the sixteenth year of our reign (i.e. 1215) and the restoration of peace.
In addition we have caused letters patent to be made for the barons, bearing witness to this security and to the concessions set out above, over the seals of Stephen archbishop of Canterbury, Henry archbishop of Dublin, the other bishops named above, and Master Pandulf.
(63) IT IS ACCORDINGLY OUR WISH AND COMMAND that the English Church shall be free, and that men in our kingdom shall have and keep all these liberties, rights, and concessions, well and peaceably in their fullness and entirety for them and their heirs, of us and our heirs, in all things and all places for ever.
Both we and the barons have sworn that all this shall be observed in good faith and without deceit. Witness the above-mentioned people and many others.
Given by our hand in the meadow that is called Runnymede, between Windsor and Staines, on the fifteenth day of June in the seventeenth year of our reign.

MAGNA CARTA (CHARTER OF RIGHTS) 1217

HENRY, by the Grace of God, King of England, Lord of Ireland, of Normandy and Aquitaine, and Earl of Anjou, to the archbishops, bishops, abbots, priors, earls, barons, sheriffs, governors, officers and all bailiffs, and his faithful subjects, who see this present charter, Greeting.
Know ye that in the presence of God, and for the salvation of our own soul, and for the souls of our ancestors, and of our successors, to the exaltation of the Holy Church, and the amendment of our kingdom,

we grant, by this present Charter we have confirmed for its and our heirs forever, by the council of our venerable fathers, the Lord Gualo, entitled a Cardinal Priest of St. Martin, Legate from the Holy See, the Lord Walter, Archbishop of York, William Bishop of London, and other Bishops of England, and William Marshal Earl of Pembroke, Guardian of us and of our kingdom, and others of our faithful earls and barons of England, these underwritten liberties to be held in our realm of England forever.

(1) in the first place we grant unto God, and by this our present Charter we have confirmed for us and for our heirs forever, that the English Church shall be fre, and shall have her whole rights, and he liberties, inviolable.

(2) We have also granted to all the free-men of our kingdom, for us and for our heirs for ever, all the underwritten liberties to be held by them and by their heirs, of us and our heirs.

(3) If any of our earls or barons, or others who hold of us in chief by military service, shall die, and at his death his heir shall be of full age, and shall owe relief, he shall have his inheritance by the ancient relief; that is to say, the heir or heirs of an earl, a whole earl's baronry for one hundred pounds: the heir or heirs of a baron, a whole baronry, for one hundred pounds; the heir or heirs of a knight, a whole knight's fee, for one hundred shillings at the most: and he who owes less, shall give less, according to the ancient customs of fees.

(4) The warden of the land of such heir who shall be under age, shall not take from the lands of the heir any but reasonable issues, and reasonable customs, and reasonable services, and that without destruction and waste of the men or goods. And if we commit the custody of any such lands to a sheriff, or any other person who is bound to us for the issues of them, and

he shall make destruction and waste of the ward-lands, we will recover damages from him, and the land shall be committed to two lawful and discreet men of the same fee, who shall answer for the issues to us, or to him to whom we have assigned them: and if we shall give or sell to anyone the custody of any such lands, and he shall make destruction or waste upon them, he shall lose the custody; and it shall be committed to two lawful and discreet men of the same fee, who shall answer to us in like manner as it is said before.

(5) But the warden, as long as he has the custody of the lands, shall keep up and maintain the houses, parks, warrens, ponds, mills and other things belonging to them, out of their issues; and shall restore to the heir, when he comes of full age, his whole estate, provided with carriages and all other things, at the least such as he received it. All these things shall be observed in the custodies of vacant archbishoprics, bishoprics, abbeys, priories, churches, and dignities, which appertain to us, excepting that these wardships are not to be sold.

(6) Heirs shall be married without disparagement. (Not to someone of a lower social status).

(7) A widow, after the death of her husband, shall immediately, and without difficulty, have her freedom of marriage and her inheritance; nor shall she give anything for her dower, or for her freedom of marriage, or for her inheritance, which her husband and she held at the day of his death; and she may remain at the principal messuage of her husband, for forty days after her husband's death, within which time here dower be assigned; unless it shall have been assigned before, or excepting his house shall be a castle; and if she depart from the castle, there shall be provided for her a complete house in which she may decently dwell, until her dower shall be assigned to her as aforesaid. And

she shall have her reasonable estover (necessary things) within a common term. And for her dower, shall be assigned to her the third part of all the lands of her husband, which were his during his life, except she were endowed with less at the church door.

(8) No widow shall be compelled to marry, whilst she is willing to dwell without a husband; but yet she shall give security that she will not marry without our consent, if she holds lands of us, or without the consent of her lord if she hold of another.

(9) Neither he nor bailiffs, will seize any land or rent for any debt, whilst the chattels of the debtor present sufficient for the payment fo the debt, and the debtor shall be ready to make satisfaction: nor shall the sureties of the debtor be distrained, whilst the principal debtor is able to pay the debt; and if the principal debtor fail in payment of the debt, not having wherewith to discharge it, or will not discharge it when he is able, then the sureties shall answer for the debt; and if they be willing, they shall have the lands and rents of the debtor, until satisfaction be made for the debt which they had before paid for him, unless the principal debtor can show himself acquitted thereof against the said sureties.

(10) The City of London shall have all its ancient liberties, and it's free customs, as well by land as by water. Furthermore, we will and grant that all other cities, burghs, and towns and the barons of the Cinque Ports, and all ports, should have all their liberties and free customs.

(11) None shall be distrained to do more service for a knight's fee, nor for any other fee tenement than what is due from thence.

(12) Common Pleas shall not follow our court, but shall be held in a fixed place.

(13) Trials upon the writs of 'novel disseisin' (recent interruption of land ownership), and of 'mort d' ancestre' (heir deprived of inheritance) shall not be taken but in their proper counties, and in this manner:-we, or our Chief Justiciary, if we should be out of the kingdom, will send justiciaries into every county, once in the year; who, with the knights of each county, shall hold in the county, the aforesaid assizes. And those things, which at the coming of the aforesaid justiciaries being sent to take the said assizes, cannot be determined, shall be ended by them in some other place in their circuit; and those things which for difficulty of some of the articles cannot be determined by them, shall be determined by our justiciaries of the Bench, and there shall be ended.
(14) Assizes of 'darrein presentment' (last person to appoint a clergyman) shall always be taken to our justiciaries of the Bench, and there shall be determined.
(15) A free-man shall not be amerced for a small offence, but only according to the degree of the offence; and for a great delinquency, according to the magnitude of the delinquency, saving his contentment: a merchant in the same manner, saving his merchandise, a villein, if he belong to another, shall be amerced after the same manner, saving him his wainage, if he shall fall into mercy; and none of the aforesaid amercements shall be assessed, but by the oath of honest and lawful men of the neighborhood. Earls and barons shall not be amerced but by their peers, and that only according to the degree of their delinquency. No ecclesiastical person shall be amerced according to the quantity of his ecclesiastical benefice, but according to the quantity of his lay-fee, and the extent of his crime.
(16) Neither a town nor any person shall be distrained to build bridges or embankments, excepting those which anciently, and of right, are bound to do it.

(17) No embankments shall from henceforth be defended, but such as were in defense in the time of King Henry our grandfather; by the same places, and the same bounds as they were accustomed to be in his time.

(18) No sheriff, constable, coroner, nor other of our bailiffs, shall hold pleas of (which should be dealt with by)our crown.

(19) If anyone holding of us a lay fee dies, and the sheriff or our bailiff shall show our letters-patent of summons concerning the debt which the deceased owed to us, it shall be lawful for the sheriff, or for our bailiff to attach and register the chattels of the deceased found on that lay fee, to the amount of that debt by the view of lawful men, so that nothing shall be removed from thence until our debt be paid to us; and the rest shall be left to the executors to fulfill the will of the deceased; and if nothing be owing to us by him, all the chattels shall fall to the deceased, saving to his wife and children their reasonable shares.

(20) No constable, governor, nor his bailiff shall take the grain or other goods of anyone, who is not of that town where the castle is, without instantly paying money for them, unless he can obtain a respite from the free will of the seller; but if he be of that town wherein the castle is, he shall give him the price within forty days.

(21) No constable shall distrain any knight to give him money for castle-guard, if he is willing to perform it in his own person, or by another able man, if he cannot perform it himself, for a reasonable cause: and if we do lead or send him into the army, he shall be excused from castle-guard, according to the time that he shall be with us in the army, on account of the fee for which he hath done service in the host.

(22) No sheriff nor bailiff of ours, nor of any other person, shall take the horses or carts of any, for the purpose of carriage, without paying according to the rate anciently appointed; that is to say, for a cart with two horses, ten-pence by the day, and for a cart with three horses, fourteen-pence by the day.

(23) No demesne cart of any ecclesiastical person, or knight, or any lord shall be taken by the aforesaid bailiffs.

(24) Neither we, nor our bailiffs, nor those of another, shall take another man's wood, for our castles or for other uses, unless by the consent of him to whom the wood belongs.

(25) We will not retain the lands of those convicted of felony, except for one year and one day, and then they shall be given up to the lord of the fee concerned.

(26) All fish weirs for the future shall be quite removed out of the Thames and the Medway, and through all England, excepting upon the sea coast.

(27) The writ which is called 'praecipe', for the future shall not be granted to anyone of any tenement, by which a free-man loses his (right of trial in his lord's) court.

(28) There shall be one measure of wine throughout all our kingdom, and one measure of ale, and one measure of grain, namely the quarter of London; and one breadth of dyed cloth, and of russets, and of halberjacks, namely two ells within the selvedges. Also it shall be the same with weights as with measures.

(29) Nothing shall for the future be given or taken for the issue of a writ of inquisition, nor taken of him that requests inquisition of life or limb; but it shall be given without charge, and not denied.

(30) If any man holds of us by fee-farm, or socage, or by burgage, and holds land of another by military service,

we will not have the guardianship of his heir, nor of his lands, which are of the fee-farm, socage, or burgage, unless the fee-farm owe military service. We will not have the custody of the man's heir, nor of the lands of anyone, which holds of another by military service, on account of any petty-sergeantry which he holds of us by the service of giving us daggers, or arrows, or the like.

(31) No bailiff, for the future, shall put any man on trial, nor to an oath, upon simple affirmation, without faithful witnesses produced for that purpose.

(32) No free-man shall be taken or imprisoned, or dispossessed, of his free tenement, or liberties, or free customs, or be outlawed, or exiled, or in any way destroyed; nor will we condemn him, nor will we commit him to prison, excepting by the legal judgement of his peers, or by the laws of the land.

(33) To none will we sell, to none will we deny, to none will we delay right or justice.

(34) All merchants, unless they have been before publically prohibited, shall have safety and security in going out of England, and in coming into England, and in staying and in traveling through England, as well as by land as by water, to buy and sell, without any unjust exactions, according to ancient right and customs, excepting in time of war, and if they be of a country at war against us: and if such be found in our land at the beginning of the war, they shall be apprehended, without injury of their bodies of goods, until it be known to us, or to our Chief justiciar, how the merchants of our country are treated who are found in the country at war against us: and if ours be in safety there, the others will be in safety in our land.

(35) If any man holds lands of any escheat, as of the honor of Wallingford, Boulogne, Nottingham, Lancaster, or of other escheats which are in our hand, and are

baronies, and shall die, his heir shall not give any other relief, nor do any other service to us, than he should have done to the baron, if those lands had been in the hands of the baron; and we will hold it in escheat, any escheat, or custody of any of our men, unless he who held the barony or escheat, held otherwise of us in chief.
(36) No free-man shall from henceforth, give or sell any more of his land, but so that of the residue of his lands, the lord of the fee may have the service due to him which belongs to the fee.
(37) All patrons of abbeys, which are held by Charters of Advowson from the Kings of England, or by ancient tenure or possession of the same, shall have the custody of them when they become vacant, as they ought to have, and such as it hath been declared above.
(38) No man shall be apprehended or imprisoned on the appeal of a woman, for the death of any man except her husband.
(39) No County Court, shall, from henceforth be held, but from month to month; and where a greater term has been used, it shall be greater. Neither shall any sheriff or his bailiff, keep his turn in the hundred but twice in the year; and nowhere but in due and accustomed place; that is to say, once after Easter, and again after the feast of St. Michael. And the view of frank-pledge shall be likewise at Saint Michael's term, without occasion: so that every man may have his liberties, which he had had and was accustomed to have, in the time of King Henry our grandfather, or which he hath since procured him. Also the new frank-pledge shall be so done, that our peace may be kept, and that the tything may be wholly kept, as it hath been accustomed; and that the sheriff seek no occasions, and that he be content with so much as the sheriff was wont to have his view-making, in the time of King Henry our grandfather. *(The frank-*

pledge is a compulsory sharing of responsibility among people sharing kinship or oath to a lord. All men over 12 years old were joined in groups of about ten households. The group leader, or tithing-man, must produce any man suspected of a crime, or the whole group could be fined).

(40) It shall not, from henceforth, be lawful for any to give his lands to any religious house, and to take the same land again to hold of the same house; nor shall it be lawful to any house of religion to take the lands of any, and to lease the same to him from whom they were received. Therefore, if any from henceforth do give his land to any religious house, and thereupon be convict, his gift shall be utterly void, and the land shall accrue to the lord of the fee.

(41) Scutage (*money instead of knight's service*) from henceforth shall be taken as it was accustomed to be taken in the time of King Henry our grandfather.

(42) Also all those customs and liberties aforesaid, which we have granted to be held in our kingdom, for so much of it as belongs to us, all our subjects, as well clergy as laity, shall observe towards their tenants as far as it concerns them.

(43) We also ordain by the common Council of our whole kingdom, that all the adulterine castles, namely those, which from the beginning of the turbulent war between the Lord John our Father, and his barons of England which were built or re-edified, shall be pulled down.

But because we have not as yet any seal, we have caused this to be sealed with the seals of our Lord the Legate aforesaid, and of the Earl William Marshal, guardian of us and our kingdom.

First Forest Charter, 1217

HENRY, by the grace of God, King of England, Lord of Ireland, Duke of Normandy, Aquitaine, and Count of Anjou, to the archbishops, bishops, abbots, priors, earls, barons. justiciaries, foresters, sheriffs, governors, officers, and all his bailiffs and faithful subjects, Greeting.

Know ye that we, for the honour for God and for the salvation of our own soul and the souls of our ancestors and successors, for the exaltation of Holy Church and the reform of our realm, have granted and by this present charter have confirmed for us and our heirs forever, by the counsel of our venerable father Lord Gualo entitled Cardinal priest of St. martin and legate of the Apostolic See, of the Lord Walter Archbishop of York, William Bishop of London and the other bishops of England and of William Marshal Earl of Pembroke, guardian of us and of our kingdom, and of others of our faithful earls and barons of England, these underwritten liberties to be held in our kingdom of England forever.

(1) First, all the forests made by our grandfather King Henry, shall be viewed by good, lawful men, and if he made any other than his own proper woods into forests to the damage of him whose woods it was, it shall forthwith be disafforested. And if he made his own proper wood forests, it shall remain forest, saving the right of pasturage, and of other things in the same forest, to those who were formerly accustomed to have them.

(2) Men who live outside the forest, from henceforth shall not come before our judiciaries of the forest, upon a common summons, unless they are impleaded there or are sureties for any other who were attached for something concerning the forest.
(3) Also all woods which were afforested by King Richard our uncle, or by King John our father, until our own first coronation, shall forthwith be disafforested, unless they shall be our demesne woods.
(4) Archbishops, bishops, abbots, priors, earls, barons, knights and freeholders who have woods within forests shall have them the same as they held them at the time of the first coronation of our grandfather King Henry, so that they shall be discouraged forever of all purprestures, wastes, and assarts made in their woods after that time until the beginning of the second year of our coronation. And those who in future shall without our license make wastes purprestures or assets within them shall answer for such wastes, purprestures, or assarts.
(5) Our regarders shall go through the forests to make a view as it was used to be made at the time of the first coronation of our grandfather, King Henry, and not otherwise.
(6) The inquisition or view for lawing of dogs living within the forest, for the future shall be when the view ought to be made, namely, the third year in three years; and then it shall be done by the view and testimony of lawful men, and not otherwise. And he whose dogs shall be found then unlawed, shall give three shillings for mercy, and for the future no one's ox shall be taken for lawing.

Such lawing also shall be done by the assize commonly used; which is, that three claws shall be cut off outside the ball of the fore-foot. Nor shall dogs be lawed from henceforth, expecting in places where it hath been customary to expedite them from the time of the first coronation of King Henry our grandfather.

(7) No forester nor beadle shall for the future make any alehouse, nor collect sheaves of wheat or oats, or any grain, or lambs or swine, nor shall make any gathering but by the view and oath of twelve regarders; and when they shall make their view: as many foresters shall be appointed to keep the forests, as they shall think reasonably sufficient for the purpose.

(8) No swainmote (forestry court) for the future shall be held in our kingdom, excepting thrice a year; namely, in the beginning of fifteen days before the Feast of St. Michael when the agistators meet for the agisting of our demesne woods; and about the Feast of St. Martin, when our agistators ought to receive our pannage-dues: and in those two swainmotes the foresters, verders, and agistators shall meet, and no others by distraint; and the third shall be held in the beginning of the fifteen days before the Feast of St. John the Baptist concerning the fawning of our does; and at that swainmote the tenants shall meet the foresters and verders, and no others shall be distrained to be there. Moreover every forty days through the whole year, the foresters and verders shall meet for seeing to attachments of the forests as well of vert as of venison, by the presentment of the foresters themselves and before those who are attached. And the aforesaid swainmotes shall not be holden, except in those counties where they were accustomed to be held.

(9) Every free-man shall agist (pasture livestock) his own wood in the forest as he wishes and have his pannage (swine forage). We grant also that every free-man may drive his swine through our demesne wood freely and without impediment to agist them in his own woods or anywhere else as he wishes. And if the swine

of any free-man shall remain one night in our forest, he shall not on that account lose anything of his for it.
(10) Mp man henceforth shall lose his life or limb for taking our venison, but if he shall be seized and convicted of taking venison he shall be fined heavily if he has the means to pay; but if he has not the means, he shall lie in our prison for a year and a day; and if after a year and a day he can find sureties, he shall leave prison; but if not, he shall abjure the kingdom of England.
(11) Whatever archbishop, bishop, earl or baron shall be passing through our forest, it shall be lawful for them to take one or two deer under the view of the forester, if he shall be present; but id not, he shall cause a horn to be blown, least it should seem like theft.
(12) Every free-man for the future, may, without being prosecuted, erect a mill in his own wood or upon his own land which he has in the forest; or make a warren, or pond, or marl-pit, or ditch, or turn it into arable land, so that it be not to the detriment of any of the neighbors.
(13) Every free-man shall have the eyries of hawks, sparrow hawks, falcons, eagles and herons in his own woods, and he shall likewise have the honey found in his woods.
(14) No forester from henceforth, who is not a forester in fee-farm, giving to us rent for his bailiwick, shall take any cheminage (toll) within his bailiwick; but a forester in fee, paying to us rent for his bailiwick, shall take cheminage; that is to say, for every cart two-pence for the one half year, and two-pence for the other half year; and for a horse that carries burdens one half-penny for the one half year, and half-penny for the other half year: not that excepting of those who come out of their bailiwick by license of their bailiff as dealers, to buy under wood, timber, bark, or charcoal; to carry it to sell in other

places where they will: and of no other carts nor burdens shall any cheminage be taken; and cheminage shall not be taken excepting in those places where anciently it used to be and ought to be taken. Also those who carry wood, bark or charcoal, upon their backs to sell, although they get their livelihood by it, shall not for the future pay cheminage. Also cheminage shall not be taken by our foresters, for any besides our demesne woods.

(15) All persons outlawed for forest offenses from the time of King Henry our grandfather up to our first coronation, shall be released from their outlawry without legal proceedings; and they shall find sureties that for the future they will not trespass unto us in our forests.

(16) No castellan or other person shall hold forest pleas whether concerning vert or venison but every forester-in-fee shall attach forest pleas as well concerning both vert and venison and shall present them to the verders of the provinces; and when they have enrolled and put under the seals of the verders they shall be presented to our chief forester, when he comes into those parts to hold forest pleas and before him they shall be determined.

And these liberties concerning the forests we have granted to al men, saving to the archbishop, bishops, abbots, priors, earls, barons, knights, and others, ecclesiastical as well as secular; Templars and Hospitallers, their liberties and free customs, in forests and outside, in warrens and other places, which they had previously. All these aforesaid customs and liberties which we have granted to be observed in our kingdom as for us much as it belongs to us; all our kingdom shall observe, clergy as well as laity, for as much as belongs to them. Because we have at present no seal, we have causes the present charter to be sealed with the seals of our venerable father Lord Gualo entitled Cardinal-priest of St. martin, Legate of the Apostolic See, and of William marshal Earl of Pembroke, guardian of us and of our kingdom. Witness the before-names and many others. Given by the hands of the aforementioned lord, the legate, and of William Marshal at St. Paul's London, on the sixth day of November in the second year of our reign.

BIBLIOGRAPHY

AuBuchon, Dennis, "Connecting the Magna Carta to the U.S. Constitution" (2014), http://dennisaubuhon.hubpages.com/hub/Connecting-the -Magna-Carta-to-the -US-Constitution. (accessed 7/14)

Baldwin, John W., *Master Stephen Langton, Future Archbishop of Canterbury: the Paris School and Magna Carta* (online 2008) Reviewed in English Historical Review (2008) CXXIII (503): http://englishhistoricalreview.org/811-846doi;10.1053/ehr/cen176 . (accessed 6/14).

Barlow, Frank, *William Rufus* (Berkeley: University of California press, 1983).

Bible, King James Version has been used throughout. Any publisher.

Bleiberg, Edward I., et al. (ed.) "Secular Clergy: Reform and Reaction", "Innocent III", Medieval *Europe 814-1450* Vol. 3. (Detroit: Gale, Cengage Learning, 2005).

Bryant, Sir Arthur, The *Medieval Foundation of England* (Garden City: Doubleday and Company, 1967).

Bye, Arthur E., *Magna Carta, King John and the Barons* (Bridgeport: Chancellor Press, 1966).

Clayton, Joseph, *Leaders of the People: Studies in Democratic History* (New York: Mitchell Kennerley, 1910).

Costain, Thomas B., *The Conquerors* (Garden City: Doubleday and Company, 1950).

Davenport Adams, William Henry, *Warrior, Priest and Statesman; or English Heroes in the Thirteenth Century*

(1845) http://books.google.com/books?=id=IWOBAAAAQAAJ . (accessed 8/14).

Daziger, Danny and Gillingham, John, *1215: the Year of Magna Carta (*London: Hodder & Sloughton, 2003) .

Durant, Will, *The Story of Civilization: the Age of Faith AD 325-1300* (New York: Simon and Schuster, 1950).

Encyclopedia of World Biography, (Detroit: Gale, 1998) www.gale.cengage.com/AcademiconeFile.com. (6/14, 2014).

Farrer, W., "An Outline Itinerary of Henry I", *English Historical Review* No. 135, (July, 1919).

Freeman, Edward A., *The History of the Norman Conquest of England,* Vol. V., (New York, AMS Press, 1977 from 1876 edition).

Green, Judith A., *Government of England under Henry I* (Cambridge: Cambridge University Press, 1986).

Grout, Donald Jay, *A History of Western Music* (New York: Norton & Company, 1960).

Hassall, W. O., *How They Lived; An Anthology of Original Accounts Written Before 1485* (Oxford: Basil Blackford, 1962).

Hollister, C. Warren, *Henry I* (New Haven: Yale University Press, 2001).

Huneycutt, Lois L., *Matilda of Scotland: a Study in Medieval Queenship* (Woodbridge: Boydell Press, 2003).

Jones, Dan *The Plantagenets: The Warrior Kings and Queens Who Made England* (New York: Viking Press, Penguin Books, 2012).

Kuiper, B. K., *The Church in History* (Grand Rapids: Wm. B. Eerdmans Publishing, 1964) .

Lacombe, George; Smalley, Beryl & Gregory, Alys, *Studies on the Commentaries of Cardinal Stephen Langton* (Archives d'Historie doctrinale et litt'eraire du Moyen Age--a reprint, c.a. 1930).

Macy, Gary "Magna Carta: Heresy!" National Catholic Reporter 36.29 (May 19, 2000): p. 20 http://ncronline.org/. (accessed 7/14).

Mordschein, Ken, "The Medieval University" http://www.renaissancemagazine.com/backissues/univ.html . (accessed 7/14)

Painter, Sidney, *William Marshal: Knight-errant, Baron & Regent of England* (Boston: Johns Hopkins Press, 1967).

Pernoud, Regine, (trans. Peter Wiles) *Eleanor of Aquitaine* (New York, Coward-McCann, 1968).

Planche', J. R., *The Conqueror and His Companions*, Volume 2, (London: Tinsley Press, 1874).

Powicke, F. M., *Stephen Langton: Being the Ford Lectures Delivered in the University of Oxford in Hillary Term 1927* (Somerset: Sandpiper Press, 1997 from Oxford University Press, 1928) .

Roberts, Phyllis Barzillay, *Studies in the Sermons of Stephen Langton* (Toronto: Pontifical Institute of Mediaeval Studies, 1968).

Round, J. H., *Feudal England* (London: Swan Sonnenschein and Co., 1909).

Saal, Nigel, *A Companion to Medieval England 1066-1485* (Stroud: Tempus Publishing, 2005).

Schaff, Philip, *History of the Church* Vol. V., (Grand Rapids: Wm. B. Eerdmans Publishing, 1974).

Schmitt, Franciscus Salesius, *Stanford Encyclopedia of Philosophy,* (1968), http://plato.stanford.edu/entries/anselm/ (accessed 7/14)

Sherman, Charles P., "The Romanization of English Law" The Yale Law Journal article

10.2307/785012 http://www.jstor.org/stable/78012 (accessed 6/14).

Stearns, Peter N. (ed), *Encyclopedia of World History, 6th edition* (New York: Houghton Mifflin Co., 2001).

Steinmeuller, John E., "History of the Latin Vulgate" http://catholicculture.org/Library/view.cfm?recnum=7470 (accessed 8/14).

Stephenson, Carl and Marcham, Frederick G., *Sources of English Constitutional History* (New York: Harper and Row, 1937).

Toovey, James, *Lives of the English Saints* Vol. 10, (1845) http://books.google.com/books?oe=UTF-8&id=aewOAAAAIAAJ&q=Langton (accessed 6/14).

Tierney, Brian and Painter, Sidney, *Western Europe in the Middle Ages 300--1475* (New York: Alfred A. Knopf, 1970).

Vaughn, Sally N. *Anselm of Bec and Robert of Meulan* (Berkeley: University of California Press, 1987

www.bsswebsite.me.uk/History/MagnaCarta/magnacarta-1217.htm (accessed 11/14) References *An Historical Essay on the Magna Carta of King John* by Richard Thomson, 1829.

www.bsswebsite.me.uk/History/MagnaCata/forestcharter-1217.htm (accessed 11/14).

www.nhinet.org/ccs/docs/char-lib.htm (accessed 11/14).

www.ingramcontent.com/pod-product-compliance
Lightning Source LLC
Chambersburg PA
CBHW020004050426
42450CB00005B/298